THE CATECHIST'S TOOLBOX 2.0

I0805929

Other Loyola Press Books by Joe Paprocki

The Catechist's Toolbox: How to Thrive as a Religious Education Teacher

A Well-Built Faith: A Catholic's Guide to Knowing and Sharing What We Believe

The Bible Blueprint: A Catholic's Guide to Understanding and Embracing God's Word

Practice Makes Catholic: Moving from a Learned Faith to a Lived Faith

Beyond the Catechist's Toolbox: Catechesis That Not Only Informs but Also Transforms

Living the Sacraments: Finding God at the Intersection of Heaven and Earth

The Catechist's Backpack: Spiritual Essentials for the Journey

Preparing Hearts and Minds: 9 Simple Ways for Catechists to Cultivate a Living Faith

Under the Influence of Jesus: The Transforming Experience of Encountering Christ

7 Keys to Spiritual Wellness: Enriching Your Faith by Strengthening the Health of Your Soul

Living the Mass: How One Hour a Week Can Change Your Life (with Fr. Dominic Grassi)

A Church on the Move: 52 Ways to Get Mission and Mercy in Motion

8 Steps to Energize Your Faith

Joe Paprocki, DMin

The Catechist's Toolbox 2.0

Building Today's Missionary Disciples

Revised and Updated

LoyolaPress.
A Jesuit Ministry

LOYOLA PRESS.
A JESUIT MINISTRY

www.loyolapress.com

Portions of this book were previously published in *Tools for Teaching: Classroom Tips for Catechists* (Mystic, CT: Twenty-third Publications, 1997).

Cover design by Loyola Press
Interior design by Loyola Press

ISBN: 978-0-8294-5885-5
Library of Congress Control Number: 2024950424

Printed in the United States of America
25 26 27 28 29 30 31 32 33 34 Versa 10 9 8 7 6 5 4 3 2 1

Dedication

To all the good folks of Loyola Press, past, present, and future,

who help so many people find God in their everyday lives.

CONTENTS

Acknowledgments

I am extremely grateful to the following people: **Joe Durepos** for creating the vision for what has become the Toolbox series; **Terry Locke** for developing the pricing plan that has enabled thousands of parishes to afford purchasing the book for all of their catechists year after year; **Gary Jansen** for recognizing the importance of moving this book into the twenty-first century; **Joellyn Cicciarelli** for numerous insightful conversations about the future of education; **Dave Gruber** for doing a thorough read-through of the manuscript to provide me with insights from a veteran professional catechetical leader; **Joe Sodini**, my best friend since the first day of high school at St. Ignatius College Prep, for asking me the $64,000 question while we enjoyed a beer on his speedboat right before I started this project: "So, how *are* learners different today than they were when you first wrote the book?"; **Maura Poston** for a remarkable job of editing my writing; **Alison Shurtz** for excellent copyediting; **Donna Antkowiak** for exquisite design; and my wonderful wife **Joanne** for generously sharing her knowledge and expertise about education and curriculum, amassed over nearly forty years as a professional educator, not to mention her love and support that never ceases—and never ceases to amaze me!

Preface: Can Robots Replace Catechists?

"Can robots replace catechists?" Some years ago, I asked this question on my blog, *The Catechist's Journey*.

Indeed, the twenty-first century has seen and will continue to see the proliferation of artificial intelligence (AI). Along with that proliferation come many questions about the appropriate use of AI. Truth be told, if catechesis is primarily about transmitting content, then we might as well let robots do the work. They would be very efficient and more consistently accurate. Catechesis, however, is not primarily about *transmitting information*; it is about *transformation*. As a catechist, you are not a teacher of a subject. Rather, you are a facilitator of transformative encounters with Jesus Christ. A robot can speak to the head. But as a catechist, you speak not only to the head, but also to the heart. Unlike you, a robot cannot give authentic witness. So the answer to the question, "Can robots replace catechists?" is a definitive *no*!

Unlike you, a robot cannot give authentic witness.

And yet, we live in a new age shaped by technology. Those we teach were born on the "digital continent" and speak its native tongue. Our task as twenty-first century catechists is to combine the very best of new technologies with good old-fashioned human warmth, wisdom, and wonder.

Robots aside, even within human ranks, please know that as a catechist, you are not easily replaced. Although there may be several hundred thousand volunteer catechists in the United States alone, that amounts to fewer than 1 percent of all the Catholics in the country. You are part of a select community of people in the Church who have been called to form disciples of Jesus Christ in a faith formation program. Through your ministry you are carrying out Jesus's Great Commission to "Go, therefore, and make disciples of all nations, . . . teaching them to observe all that I have commanded you" (Matthew 28:19–20).

Thank you for all that you do to proclaim the Good News of Jesus Christ!

God's
Raw
Material
HALL

Introduction: New Tools for New Mentalities

For home improvements, new tools are often lighter, faster, and more efficient, durable, powerful, versatile, and ergonomic. Likewise, catechists benefit from new tools to meet new challenges.

New Mentalities

> **[The ecclesial community] will be eager to get inside those junctures of existence, anthropological environments, and modern areopagi where cultural tendencies are created and new mentalities are shaped.**
>
> —*Directory for Catechesis*, 324

So . . . why the need for an updated retooled edition of this book? *The Catechist's Toolbox* first appeared on the scene in 2007, a year in which many significant things occurred in pop history: Prince performed at the Super Bowl halftime show; Tiger Woods won his fourth PGA Championship; *The Sopranos* TV show came to an end while *Keeping Up with the Kardashians* premiered; R.E.M. was voted into the Rock & Roll Hall of Fame; and Barry Bonds surpassed Hank Aaron as the all-time MLB home run leader. Most significantly, however, in 2007, Steve Jobs and Apple introduced the iPhone, which enabled people to carry with them a multimedia device that was not only a phone but also an MP3 player and Internet browser. And the world has not been the same since.

Why was this technological milestone so significant? In her book *Generations*, researcher, psychology professor, and author Dr. Jean Twenge asserts that generational behaviors and attitudes are most significantly shaped by technological advances, even more so than other seismic events such as war, a terrorist attack, or an economic crisis such as the Great Depression. And few technological advances have had as immediate, momentous, and significant an impact as the smartphone and social media, which exploded onto the scene in 2007.

According to Twenge, "The smartphone brought about a planetary rewiring of human interaction. As smartphones became common, they transformed peer relationships, family relationships and the texture of daily life for everyone" (Haidt and Twenge, 2021). The impact that smartphone technology has had on learning in the twenty-first century has been and will continue to be profound. In essence, how we think and learn has changed. Learners' brains have been rewired in a number of ways. So, as catechists, what new tools do we need to address new mentalities?

In essence, how we think and learn has changed. Learners' brains have been rewired in a number of ways.

Retooling the Catechist's Toolbox

In response to these changes in how we think and learn, those who teach, including catechists, must retool to effectively engage the minds and hearts of learners in the twenty-first century. Long gone is the one-size-fits-all approach of the early twentieth-century *Baltimore Catechism* (which served well for a world that ceased to exist decades ago), where the catechist was the source of all knowledge and students were expected to passively absorb information like a sponge.

The Four Cs of Twenty-First Century Learning Skills

In 2002, the Partnership for 21st Century Learning, a collaboration of teachers, education experts, and business leaders that is also known as P21, was formed to put twenty-first century skills at the center of learning. As part of their work, P21 has identified four broad categories of life skills and personality traits that young people will need to succeed in the twenty-first century. Known as the Four Cs, these skills are:

- Collaboration
- Communication
- Creativity
- Critical Thinking

BECAUSE twenty-first century learners . . .

- **. . . are accustomed to switching tasks frequently** and find it difficult to avoid distractions and maintain attention for longer periods of intense concentration, *catechists must respond* by "chunking"—dividing faith formation sessions into a variety of eight- to ten-minute chunks of time and incorporating various learning activities that allow for a shift in energy and enable learners to maintain attention. Displaying a brief agenda or lesson plan for the session can help learners prepare mentally for and get excited about the variety of things they'll be doing.
- **. . . are accustomed to intense visual and audio stimuli,** *catechists must respond* by regularly integrating informative audiovisual information and inspiration through multiple forms of media to effectively capture the imagination and attention of learners.
- **. . . are accustomed to instant, easy access to abundant information and content,** *catechists must respond* by occasionally allowing the use of smartphones or tablets to access content. In addition, catechists can utilize a flipped classroom approach that invites learners to access content before the faith formation session so that the session itself can provide ample opportunities (such as through small groups working on projects, discussing essential questions, or praying together) for learners to apply content to their daily lives and to reflect on how God is active in their lives.

"Your furnace is pretty outdated. I can see the footprints of Shadrach, Meshach, and Abednego."

- **. . . are more demanding and critical of the learning experiences they participate in,** *catechists must respond* by giving options and choices with regard to learning activities while also giving learners opportunities to give feedback on the activity(ies) they most enjoy and find most helpful.
- **. . . expect their learning experiences to be customized to meet their needs,** *catechists must respond* by providing opportunities for learners to identify and share their learning styles (see chapter 6). Catechists can also permit learners to present their work in uniquely personalized ways, including digital storytelling, podcasts, infographics, photo essays, slide presentations, artistic expression, and so on.

Catechists must respond by providing opportunities for learners to identify and share their learning styles.

- **. . . face greater uncertainty because of the rapidity of change in the world,** *catechists must respond* by identifying and affirming learners' gifts and talents while encouraging them to focus on hope, confidence, and trusting that God's plan for them is to prosper. In addition, catechists can offer accompaniment while inviting learners to encounter/enter into mystery as a reality that includes uncertainty but invites a deeper experience of life.
- **. . . are exposed to social fragmentation and polarization,** *catechists must respond* by emphasizing solidarity and common ground. Likewise, to increase a sense of connectivity to the larger society, catechists can arrange for virtual (video or Zoom) or real-life access to experts (guest speakers from the parish, community, diocese, world) on themes they are exploring in their faith formation sessions.
- **. . . expect to interact with content and expect the content to be relevant and useful in their daily lives,** *catechists must respond* by giving learners time to both reflect on what they can "do" with what they're learning and also grapple with open-ended essential questions about how what they're learning relates to the real world and their real lives. Catechists can also encourage the use of technology to

Jesus and Satan were arguing about who had more computer proficiency. God the Father was tired of all the bickering and said, "Let's settle this once and for all. You each have sixty minutes to reveal all your computer skills. Ready? Go!" The two typed away feverishly at their keyboards for fifty-nine minutes, but then the power went out. Satan cursed furiously, but Jesus just sighed and sat calmly until the power came back on. Each restarted their computers, but Satan started screaming frantically, "Oh no! I lost everything when the power went out!" Meanwhile, Jesus calmly started printing out all the work he had completed. Satan observed this and became irate, yelling, "Wait! He cheated—how did he do it?" God the Father smiled, shrugged, and said, "Jesus saves."

enable learners to put their work out into the world. Examples include sharing ideas, projects, and achievements with a larger audience such as their parish, local community, or another parish or school in another part of the country or even the world.

> **If we teach today as we taught yesterday, we rob our children of tomorrow.**
> —John Dewey

- **. . . often feel alone and disconnected** (for many different reasons including family situations, self-esteem issues, bullying, fear, lack of authentic relationships, and so on), *catechists must respond* by creating and maintaining an authentic welcoming community, and then allowing learners to engage with each other in pairs or small groups on short tasks (cooperative learning, or collaboration). In addition, catechists can view learners as young "peers" whom they are called to accompany, mentor, and apprentice along the journey rather than seeing them as students who are to be taught a subject. Catechetical programs can also gravitate toward faith formation approaches that involve families rather than adhering to the traditional school model.

- **. . . consider artificial intelligence (AI) as a normative part of their cognitive process,** *catechists must respond* by providing both the necessary principles for critical thinking, decision-making, and discernment as well as opportunities to put such principles into practice.
- **. . . are experiencing digital burnout or overload,** *catechists must respond* by providing multimodal learning that includes breaks from screen time, including making connections with nature, encounters with beauty in the form of art and music, quiet time, creative expression, and reading/engaging with print materials and other tactile resources.
- **. . . are exposed to seemingly endless sources of information that may not be dependable,** *catechists must respond* by identifying reliable and trustworthy sources of information about the Catholic faith and by providing a life-giving narrative that is shared by all followers of Jesus Christ.

The Catechist's Toolbox 2.0 is not a call to make faith formation a digital reality, nor is it a nostalgic call to get rid of technology and return to simpler times. Rather, it is a call to recognize how technology is creating new ways of learning and how we as catechists need effective strategies—tools—to address these new realities and to deepen encounters with Jesus Christ while guarding against some of technology's more harmful or even toxic effects.

As catechists, we are called to forge deeper into the twenty-first century, confident that the Holy Spirit provides us with the tools we need to effectively proclaim the Good News of Jesus to today's learners. Thank you for responding to God's call to serve as a catechist! Now, let's roll up our sleeves and get to work . . . and let God get to work on us!

Chapter One

Shoptalk: The Language of Catechesis

When looking for a gizmo, gadget, or thingamajig at the local home improvement or hardware store, it helps to know the correct name of the tool you need. Likewise, as a catechist, it is good to know the language of faith formation.

Knowing the Language of Faith Formation

> **The Church teaches us the language of faith in order to introduce us to the understanding and the life of faith.**
>
> —*Directory for Catechesis*, 204

Home improvement has a language of its own. The same is true of faith formation. In fact, in many ways, the Church has a language of its own. For our purposes, we need to become more familiar with the language of faith formation, or catechetical language. Even as we move deeper into the twenty-first century and have new words being added to our vocabulary all the time (I saw the word *qubit* for the first time recently . . . and I still can't tell you what it means!), much of the language of faith formation is actually quite ancient, even if the words seem new to us.

The Church seems to like big words. Here are a few you probably don't use in everyday conversation:

- Ecclesiology
- Evangelization
- Magisterium
- Transubstantiation
- Episcopacy
- Sanctification
- Ecumenism

Do you know what CCD stands for?

Confraternity of Christian Doctrine

In decades past, the Church did such a good job of teaching a language of faith formation for children—CCD—that we are still having a difficult time putting that acronym to rest, even though few people even know what the letters stand for. (For the answer, see the upside-down feature to the side.)

In recent years, the Church has been emphasizing a different set of words, including *kerygma*, *catechesis*, *evangelization*, *mystagogy*, and *missionary discipleship*, in relation to faith formation or religious education. Notice that I did not refer to these words as new. The fact is, the words the Church is now using when it comes to faith formation have been around for centuries. They may seem new to many of us, but to the Church, they are more like family heirlooms.

Let's start our vocabulary lesson with the words listed in the graphic below.

It doesn't take a rocket scientist to realize that all these words derive from the same root word—the Greek word *katakein*, meaning "to echo" or "to sound again." When one person echoes another, it means that he or she is imitating or reflecting back what was said or done.

So what do each of these words mean?

CATECHISM

CATECHESIS

CATECHUMEN

CATECHUMENATE

CATECHIST

- A **catechism** is a written summary of the Church's understanding of God's word as revealed through Scripture and Tradition. In a sense, a catechism is the *what* of our beliefs as Catholics. In recent centuries, it was customary for children to learn their catechism using a question-and-answer format known as the *Baltimore Catechism*. Today, the *Catechism of the Catholic Church* (2000) is the official source intended as the principal reference for bishops and catechetical ministers for Catholic doctrine.

> **By words we learn thoughts, and by thoughts we learn life.**
> —Jean Baptiste Girard

- **Catechesis** is the process of transmitting the gospel. To help us understand this process, the Church has given us the *Directory for Catechesis* (2020) and the *National Directory for Catechesis* (2005). These Church documents help us to understand *how* we form people in faith.
- A **catechumen** is an adult (or child of catechetical age, generally considered the age of seven) who is preparing to receive the sacrament of baptism. Under the guidance of catechists and sponsors, catechumens engage in a process of preparation over an appropriate period of time (usually one or two years) leading to the celebration of baptism, confirmation, and Eucharist at the Easter Vigil on Holy Saturday.
- The **catechumenate** is the formal period of preparation for catechumens who are preparing for the sacraments of initiation—baptism, confirmation, and the Eucharist. Through the catechumenate (also known as the OCIA; on the next page, see the side feature "Ever heard of the OCIA?"), those preparing for initiation into the Church receive formation and catechesis from catechists and sponsors, who help them enter more deeply into the Catholic way of life.
- A **catechist** is a person (like you!) who is called by the Church to facilitate the process of faith formation in either a parish catechetical program or a Catholic school. Catechists help adults, families, adolescents, and children live lives of discipleship.

WHATEVER HAPPENED TO CCD?

So, why use the term *catechesis* when people grew so accustomed to using the term *CCD*? The fact is, CCD primarily referred to something that was for children, as well as something that one completes after a given time of study. Today, we have retrieved the notion of *catechesis* to capture the broader mission of the Church to proclaim the gospel to all people—adults, youth, and children—in order to "put people in communion with Jesus Christ" (*Catechism of the Catholic Church*, 426), which is a lifelong task.

In recent decades, the Church has made it quite clear that to be a catechist is to have a vocation. The *Directory for Catechesis* tells us, "The catechist is a Christian who receives a particular calling from God that, when accepted in faith, empowers him for the service of the transmission of faith and for the task of initiating others into the Christian life" (*DC*, 112). Throughout this book, I use the term *catechist* to refer to those who serve in the parish religious education program as well as those who serve as teachers of religion in Catholic schools.

Ever heard of the OCIA?

This acronym stands for the *Order of Christian Initiation of Adults*. The OCIA is another name for the catechumenate.

The Instituted Ministry of Catechist

In 2021, Pope Francis, in an effort to heighten awareness of the importance of catechesis, announced that the role of catechist is now to be recognized as a formal instituted ministry in the Church. In the United States, not everyone who serves as a parish catechist is called to be formally recognized in the instituted ministry of catechist. Rather, those people recognized by the bishop as having leadership roles in catechetical ministry (and having fulfilled formation requirements for such a role) are called to be recognized in this formal manner. The presence of a formal, instituted Ministry of Catechist in the diocese does not preclude using the term *catechist* for all those who, like you, serve in this role in the parish (whether parish religious education or Catholic school teachers), nor should it end the practice of parishes commissioning all catechists at the beginning of the catechetical year (usually on Catechetical Sunday, which, in the United States, is the third Sunday of September).

If you are a Catholic schoolteacher, you are responsible for teaching a variety of subjects throughout the day. Faith formation, however, is more than a subject to be taught—it is an opportunity to facilitate encounters with Christ. By referring to you as a catechist, I want to recognize and affirm your vocation to form disciples of Jesus. To be referred to as a catechist is an honor that the Church bestows only on those who pursue this vocation.

Faith formation, however, is more than a subject to be taught—it is an opportunity to facilitate encounters with Christ.

A Catechist's Role Description

As a twenty-first-century learner yourself, you'll enjoy scanning this QR code to view a brief video of Joe sharing an example of a catechist's role description.

A Few More Words to Learn: Missionary Discipleship, Evangelization, Kerygma, and Mystagogy

Before we venture further, there are a few more words that every catechist should include in their faith formation vocabulary.

- **Missionary Discipleship**—*Missionary discipleship* is a lifestyle characterized by an intentional commitment to walk with Jesus and invite others to do so. It is not so much about what you do as it is about who you are. As catechists, our primary objective is to form missionary disciples—to call others to a lifestyle change that places Jesus at the center of their lives. To be missionary is to have an outward focus, meaning that discipleship is not a "me and Jesus" reality but rather a call to bring God's mercy and compassion to others, especially those in need.
- **Evangelization**—*Evangelization* is an invitation to have one's life transformed by an ever-deepening relationship with Jesus Christ. This is an ongoing process, not a once-and-done experience, for all followers of Jesus. Nor is it a program to increase church attendance at the parish. Evangelization and catechesis go hand in hand. As catechists, we are always about the task of inviting others to deepen their relationship with Jesus (evangelization), and one of the ways we deepen a relationship with anyone is by learning more about them (catechesis). In essence, evangelization without catechesis would just be a feel-good experience, while catechesis without evangelization would be lifeless and without purpose.
- **Kerygma**—The *kerygma* (ki-RIG-muh) is the core message of the gospel: that through the life, words, and actions (especially the death and Resurrection) of Jesus Christ, the Son of God, we are rescued from sin, restored to our relationship with the Father, and reassured of the presence of the Holy Spirit. I call these the three Rs of our salvation narrative: rescue, restoration, and reassurance. It is the Good News in a nutshell. All of our teaching flows from the kerygma and must contain

The Church exists in order to evangelize.
—Pope Paul VI

A young man attended a retreat at his parish and got fired up about evangelization. When he went back to work at the horse stable where he gave riding lessons, he decided he could evangelize the folks who came for riding lessons. So he taught all the horses to gallop when he said, "Praise the Lord!" and to stop when he said, "Amen!" Those riding with him were amazed to see their horses gallop when he called out, "Praise the Lord!" and come to a stop when he called out, "Amen!" At one point, however, when the young man noticed that the horses were leading the group too close to the edge of a cliff on a narrow mountain trail, the young man hurriedly yelled, "Whoa!" but the horses kept going. Then he remembered and called out, "Amen!" Thankfully, the horses stopped just short of the edge. That is, until a relieved and thankful rider called out, "Praise the Lord!"

and communicate the spirit of the kerygma. In other words, as catechists, we are called to be "kerygmatic." Think of the kerygma as your elevator pitch—the most concise way you could answer the question, "So what *is* the Good News?" within the time frame of riding an elevator (usually less than thirty seconds).

⊕ **Mystagogy**—*Mystagogy* (MISS-tuh-go-ghee) simply means "reflection on mystery." In short, the emphasis on mystagogy is a reminder that we are not teachers of a subject but rather are facilitators of an encounter with Divine Mystery. When mystagogy is practiced in faith formation, the experience looks and feels less like a classroom (less academic) and more like a liturgical experience that includes Scripture, reflection, sharing, music and singing, sign, symbol, ritual, movement, gesture, and silence—all of which are elements of what I like to call a "language of mystery." It also means that, as a catechist, you are not only a teacher, you are also a *mystagogue*, or someone who leads others into mystery. More about both in ensuing chapters.

As a catechist, you are not only a teacher, you are also a *mystagogue*.

John 3:16

One of the most popular examples of a kerygmatic statement can be found in John 3:16—"For God so loved the world that he gave his only Son, so that everyone who believes in him might not perish but might have eternal life." Bam! First floor! Going up!

Expanding Our Vocabulary

Words are immensely powerful. The Gospel of John refers to Jesus as "the Word" that "became flesh" (John 1:14). The language of faith formation is not just a matter of semantics. By using the most appropriate words to describe who we are and what we do, we deepen our own understanding of our share in Jesus's ministry. As catechists, we partner with pastors and bishops in guiding people to a living faith. This living faith has a language all its own. We can begin to learn the language of faith by referring to who we are and what we do with the proper terms.

"As you see on your handouts, today's topic is original sin."

Scripture

In the beginning was the Word, and the Word was with God, and the Word was God. . . . And the Word became flesh and made his dwelling among us, and we saw his glory, the glory as of the Father's only Son, full of grace and truth. JOHN 1:1, 14

Prayer

Lord Jesus, Word made flesh, thank you for inviting me to proclaim you to others. Thank you for filling my life with your word. Help me speak a language of faith that will help others recognize you in their lives and deepen their relationship with you. May your word echo within my heart and within the hearts of those I teach. Amen.

Chapter Two

Blueprints: Planning and Preparation

A builder would never attempt to construct a house without first looking at the blueprints. As catechists, if we are going to build a foundation of faith for those we teach, we must prepare and follow a plan.

Planning and Preparation in Catechesis

> **The pedagogical formation of the catechist should develop several attitudes in him including . . . the capacity to prepare an itinerary of faith.**
>
> —*Directory for Catechesis*, 149E

Some of the most important work that a catechist does takes place before he or she sets foot in the learning space. Planning and preparation—which do not hinder spontaneity but rather enhance and even anticipate it—create a structure, pattern, and flow for a faith formation experience.

Preparing and planning your faith formation experience can be thought of like preparing to have guests for a special dinner. You would plan out the menu; go food shopping; check that you have enough plates, cups, and silverware for everyone who will attend; arrange the table; put out appetizers; provide drinks; and decide what to wear. You may even plan a few topics of conversation! If our guests arrived for dinner and found us running around at the last minute throwing things together on the table and looking through the freezer to find something to toss in the microwave, the success of the evening—and the state of our friendships—would be in jeopardy.

Putting in the Hours

Surveys show that the average full-time teacher puts in between ten and fifteen hours per week preparing lessons. By comparison, then, a catechist should put in between one and two hours of planning per week for teaching one weekly session. With today's technology, catechists can do much of this preparation on interactive Web sites provided by the publisher of their catechetical curriculum.

When we entertain, we do all the planning and preparation because we want our guests to know that we care about them and delight in their presence. The same approach should be kept in mind when preparing and planning as a catechist. We want to communicate to those we teach that something incredibly special is about to happen here. Likewise, we want them to know that we care about them and value the relationship we share with them.

Why couldn't Noah catch many fish?

He didn't plan ahead. He only brought two worms.

As a student teacher, I was taught that planning and preparation make up 70 percent of the total act of teaching a lesson. Of course, there may be no way to accurately prove that percentage, but after many years of teaching and serving as a catechist, I have personally found it to be a very valid estimate.

Thorough planning and preparation create a framework for the catechist to move forward in the most effective manner, while avoiding or preempting many problems, especially in maintaining discipline. An effective catechist examines the blueprint for the lesson, visualizes every possible scenario, and prepares for it. Let's take a closer look at preparation and planning.

Planning and preparation make up 70 percent of the total act of teaching a lesson.

- **Long-Range Planning**—Each session you plan is only part of an overarching plan for the whole year. Make sure you get a sense of the whole calendar year and, even more important, the Church's liturgical year, to see how all the pieces fit into the bigger picture. Anticipate how each lesson can connect with the seasons and feasts of the liturgical year as well as how each lesson can build from the previous one and lay a foundation for the next.

- **Become Familiar with the Catechetical Resource(s) You'll Be Using—**Do a deep dive into the resources you will be using (text series, video series, online resources, etc.), especially their philosophy, strategies, approaches, strengths, and weaknesses. Zero in on a set of lessons or a unit to see how each lesson fits in with the whole program.
- **Get to Know Your Learners—**Learn about the age group you will be teaching and adjust as needed to meet their unique needs. Here's a quick look at characteristics of various age groups:
  - **Early Childhood (ages 3-5), preschool and kindergarten—**In general, children at this age learn through their senses; are enormously curious; love to ask questions; have vivid imaginations; love to sing, move, rhyme, and dance; need structure and routine; have rapidly expanding cognitive abilities but short attention spans; and express themselves symbolically through play as well as through color and design.
  - **Primary Grades (ages 6-9), grades 1 through 3—**In general, children at this age are filled with curiosity and are eager to explore the world around them; are experiencing rapid growth and have boundless energy; have endless imaginations and a natural sense of wonder; are just beginning to form a conscience; are the center of their own world; are motivated to do good and avoid punishment; need a good deal of affirmation, security, and structure; are capable of reflecting for brief periods of time; can take simple prayers to heart (to memory) and can pray spontaneously; and are naturally drawn to ritual.
  - **Intermediate Grades (ages 9-11), grades 4 through 6—**Children at these ages are less literal and less fantasy-oriented; are experiencing rapid cognitive growth; are highly influenced by their peers; are into "hero worship"; tend to be rabid readers; are more aware of adult issues and current events; tend to be idealistic and concerned about fairness; are eager to be helpful to others; want to please their parents and enjoy family time but are also growing in independence; are capable of reflecting for slightly longer periods of time; are more prone to bullying; and are becoming obsessed with self-identity and self-image.

- **Junior High (ages 12-14), grades 7 and 8—**Young people at this age experience rapid growth and profound changes (both physically and emotionally); can be awkward socially and physically; can be inconsistent, moody, and jumpy; need support, guidance, attention, and reassurance; are capable of abstract thought and critical thinking; are beginning to discern gifts, talents, and even vocation; are easily bored and distracted and tend to "push the envelope"; are hungry for active learning experiences; begin to reject childhood notions of faith; are grappling with more complex moral issues and decisions; want guidance and yet push back against authority; are increasingly paradoxical (e.g., wanting freedom but needing and craving structure); and respond well to being treated as adults.

Junior highs will cheerfully comply with their leaders' requests not to stand on the chairs.

- **High School (ages 14-18), grades 9 through 12—**Most young people at this age are moving from concrete to abstract thinking; are developing the capacity to be self-reflective; are experimenting and exploring; are in search of identity; are influenced by peers and by popular culture; fluctuate between a demand for independence and a need for guidance; experience mood swings as well as swings from restlessness to fatigue to increased energy; have a developing sexual awareness; are preoccupied with changes in body size and shape; are eager for change and impatient with the pace of it; often perceive their own problems, feelings, and experiences as being unique to themselves; often lack impulse control; and make decisions based on feelings rather than a rational thought process.

Adolescence is not a pathology we must combat. It is a normal, natural part of growing up, of the life of our young people.

—Pope Francis
(*Directory for Catechesis*, 248)

Understanding Adolescents

Science teaches us that, as adolescents mature, their brains go through intensive remodeling, and the last part of the brain to develop is the prefrontal cortex, which is the decision-making part of the brain. As a result, when it comes to making decisions, teens tend to rely on the part of the brain that is associated with emotions and impulses. As a catechist, this knowledge can help you understand the behavior of teens, which can often be impulsive and lacking in awareness of consequences, while, at the same time, you are helping to lay the foundation for this very development to take place.

- **Adult—**In general, adult learners are self-directed; desire ownership of their learning experiences; expect practical, real-life connections to all learning; expect to grow and see tangible results from learning; expect to achieve a specific goal and learn things that will help them cope with life tasks and life changes; do not want to be "talked at" but prefer experiential learning; prefer to engage in meaningful conversation and meaningful action; expect to be treated as equals; expect to be invited to share their wisdom and experience; and expect learning to be a social experience that affords them an opportunity to interact with others.

Examine the Leader Materials and Ancillary Online Resources—A leader guide or catechist manual is often a catechist's best friend. Most catechetical programs provide leader resources or catechist manuals that lay out the lesson and offer step-by-step instructions. The more you familiarize yourself with the leader resources as well as ancillary online resources, the better you will be able to facilitate your session and still leave room for spontaneity.

Pray—As you sit down to plan a session, take some time to pause and ask the Holy Spirit to guide you. Do your planning and preparation in a prayerful environment. Light a candle. Put on some instrumental music. Place a Bible on the table next to you. Ask the Holy Spirit to inspire and guide you, and to give you the help you need to be focused, loving, and creative.

Do your planning and preparation in a prayerful environment.

- **Identify the *Big Idea* of Your Session**—As you do your planning, a good question to ask yourself is *What's the Big Idea?* of your session. In most cases, you can find the Big Idea stated clearly in your catechist's manual or leader guide, often embedded in the chapter title or theme. Once you know what your one-sentence Big Idea is, you'll be able to announce it to your learners and return to it over and over throughout the lesson so that learners can repeat it to their parents when they are asked to share a takeaway from the lesson. Find ways to announce the Big Idea of your session boldly, clearly, and repetitively, writing it on the board, including it in the PowerPoint presentation, printing it on handouts, and, of course, returning to it as your discussion progresses.
- **Know Your Learning Outcomes**—Have a clear knowledge of what your learners are supposed to know and be able to do because of the session. Learning outcomes focus on what the *learners* will know and do, not on what *you* are going to do. Likewise, they must be stated in measurable terms so that you will be able to assess whether the outcomes have been achieved or not. (For more on learning outcomes, see chapter 7.)
- **Prepare to Follow a Catechetical Process**—Think of your session as a movement: you want to move your learners from where they are to where Jesus invites them to be. This movement, called the *catechetical process*, involves four steps (drawn from the *Finding God* curriculum by Loyola Press):

  1. *Engage* the life experiences of the learners.
  2. *Explore* the concepts and content.
  3. *Reflect* prayerfully on how the concepts connect with life experience.
  4. *Respond* with ideas and strategies for a new way of living.

  Simply put, you take learners from where they are and move them closer to Jesus. St. Ignatius of Loyola described this as "enter through their door but be sure to leave through your door," which means a "door" that enables them to step closer to Jesus. More about the catechetical process in chapter 4, "Assembly Instructions: The Catechetical Process."

Ignatius the Catechist

St. Ignatius, who believed firmly in the importance of education, and especially education in the faith, often assumed the role of catechist. He would stand on a street corner ringing a bell to summon children for their catechism lesson!

If you don't know where you are going, you'll end up someplace else.
—Yogi Berra

- **Visualize Yourself Leading the Session—**Use your imagination to visualize the session you are preparing to lead. Imagine every possible scenario and your reactions. Keep a notepad to jot down thoughts or ideas that can now become part of your overall plan. Write down a list of materials you will need for certain situations and activities. Imagine problems that might arise and visualize how you may best handle them. With this visualization complete, you will feel as though you've already led this session once and are now building upon it.
- **Get Your Materials Ready—**Be sure that you have all the materials you will need to facilitate the session effectively. There's nothing worse than reaching a point in the session when you tell learners to cut pictures out of magazines only to find out that you don't have scissors (or magazines).
- **Have Plan B Ready—**In the course of visualizing the session ahead of time, you may discover that what you're hoping to accomplish may not work. Always have another option ready in case something falls flat or just isn't working the way you hoped it would. Develop the habit of taking notes afterward about what worked and what didn't work so that next time you can be more effective.

The Catechist's PhD: It's not unusual to see catechists heading to their learning space laden down with supplies and resources. A catechist I know once referred to this as her PhD: Pull, Haul, and Drag!

Catechetical Drop Cloths

Scan this QR code to view a brief video of Joe describing the top ten things that can and will go wrong in a typical faith formation session, as well as quick tips for how to anticipate, deal with, and prevent them.

Good Planning and Preparation Increase Confidence

Good planning and preparation for your faith formation sessions will enable you to approach the experience with calm confidence. While it's natural to be a bit nervous before getting up in front of a group, your anxiety can be lessened dramatically when you equip yourself with a well-planned session. Oh, and one more reason to plan and prepare well: the gospel and God's people deserve nothing less!

Oh, and one more reason to plan and prepare well: the gospel and God's people deserve nothing less!

Scripture

Everyone who listens to these words of mine and acts on them will be like a wise man who built his house on rock. The rain fell, the floods came, and the winds blew and buffeted the house. But it did not collapse; it had been set solidly on rock. And everyone who listens to these words of mine but does not act on them will be like a fool who built his house on sand. The rain fell, the floods came, and the winds blew and buffeted the house. And it collapsed and was completely ruined. MATTHEW 7:24–27

Prayer

Lord Jesus, our teacher, help me build my lessons upon the solid rock foundation of good planning and preparation. And when the wind comes and the rains buffet, may my teaching withstand the challenges so that those I teach may come to know that your word will endure all things, for you are Lord forever and ever. Amen.

Chapter Three

Infrared Thermometer: Creating the Right Climate

Many materials used in home improvement projects (paint, sealants, concrete, and so on) require the right conditions, such as temperature and humidity, to work properly. This is when an infrared thermometer comes in handy. Similarly, when it comes to faith formation, it is important to make sure that you have established a "climate" that is conducive to an encounter with the sacred.

> **When catechesis is permeated by a climate of prayer, the assimilation of the entire Christian life reaches its summit.**
>
> —*Directory for Catechesis*, 86

Creating the Right Climate

Weather **refers to current atmospheric conditions,** which can change in the short term. *Climate*, on the other hand, refers to a pattern of conditions over a long period of time in a certain area. These days, of course, many are rightly concerned about climate change and how it is affecting our world. There is one type of "climate change" that every catechist should be in favor of, and that is the responsibility of creating the proper climate to facilitate encounters with the risen Lord.

So how do we as catechists create a climate for divine encounters?

It All Begins with Trust

In a popular TED talk, "Why Good Leaders Make You Feel Safe," management theorist Simon Sinek emphasizes that when people feel secure and within a circle of trust, remarkable things can happen: "When we feel safe inside the organization, we will naturally combine our talents and our strengths and work tirelessly to face the dangers outside and seize the opportunities." As catechists and evangelizers, we establish trust by being authentic: by speaking credibly, acting reliably, being approachable, and focusing on the needs of others.

As catechists and evangelizers, we establish trust by being authentic: by speaking credibly, acting reliably, being approachable, and focusing on the needs of others.

How to Establish Trust

- Clearly articulate and clarify the expected behaviors for everyone, including yourself.
- Consistently, fairly, and gently confront violations of such behaviors, in private whenever possible, and then follow through by affirming the expectation.
- Encourage and protect expression of thoughts and feelings.
- Encourage and embrace openness and honesty.
- Encourage risk-taking, exploration, and curiosity without the fear of failure or disagreement.
- Incorporate cooperative learning opportunities.
- Share responsibilities.
- Show compassion and empathy.
- Celebrate diversity.
- Admit your own mistakes, shortcomings, and limitations.
- Make yourself available (within reason).
- Generously offer affirmation.
- Respect and enforce physical, emotional, and behavioral boundaries that create and ensure a safe environment.

People don't care how much you know until they know how much you care.

—Theodore Roosevelt

Preparing the Learning Space

One of the ways you create the proper climate for faith formation is by preparing the physical learning space, to the extent that you are able, to make it more conducive to an encounter with Christ. Here are some tips:

- **Remove Distractions and Clutter**—At home, work, or school, we can be easily distracted when we are surrounded by too much busyness and clutter. A clean and organized faith formation space supports positive feelings and good behavior. It is to your own benefit to arrive early and tidy up your learning space to help everyone to maintain their focus.
- **Provide a Welcoming Seating Arrangement**—If possible, arrange seating in a circle or semicircle rather than in rows; in other words, in an arrangement that encourages interaction and is also conducive to prayer. Your goal should be to create an arrangement that keeps order but also communicates a sense of hospitality and community while feeling less academic, less like a classroom.
- **Provide Name Tags or Tent Cards**—Knowing and using the names of your learners is a way of honoring them and letting them know that you really are interested in them as individuals. With young learners, it is also a way of keeping order within your faith formation space. If a learner is misbehaving, it helps to be able to call him or her by name rather than pointing and saying "Hey, you!"

Knowing and using the names of your learners is a way of honoring them and letting them know that you really are interested in them as individuals.

Ambience Matters

Relationship experts tell us that when couples plan a romantic dinner, one of the most important considerations is an ambience that encourages intimacy by allowing them to tune out distractions and focus solely on their beloved. True intimacy does not happen haphazardly but requires intentional planning. As catechists, we are called to provide settings in which our learners can truly encounter the risen Christ, who sees each one of us as a beloved disciple.

Setting Up the Prayer Center as a Ritual Action

Scan this QR code to view a brief video of Joe setting up a prayer center.

- **Create a Prayer Center**—In a faith formation setting, the central focus of your space should be Jesus. The best way to do this is to create a prayer center (aka a prayer table or prayer space), to which we alluded in chapter 2. This space communicates a "language of mystery," which we will talk about later in this chapter. What might you place in the prayer center? Consider the following:
    - a prayer cloth that reflects the color of the liturgical season
    - a Bible on a Bible stand
    - a crucifix
    - a candle (preferably flameless)
    - an icon or statuette
    - a plant or flower
    - a bowl of holy water
    - seasonal symbols (for example, an Advent wreath)
- **Display Images, Sacred Art, and Sacred Objects**—Twenty-first century learners are more visual than previous generations. Take advantage of this by displaying images and sacred art that tell stories from Scripture and the lives of the saints, help in establishing a climate of prayer, reinforce your lesson, and speak to the hearts of learners.
- **Post or Display Key Phrases**—Arrive early and write, post, and display key phrases, directions, names, and definitions on the board, easel, or SMART Board. Or, if you are using a PowerPoint presentation, be sure to include these key phrases in your slides. This way, you can refer to these images without having to turn your back to your learners to write them down.
- **Use a Language of Mystery**—If you wanted to create a climate of romance, speaking a few words in French might be in order. In the

world of faith formation, we rely on a unique language—what I call a "language of mystery"—to create and communicate a climate of prayer. It is a language that we most often use at Mass that goes beyond words and enables our sessions to resemble the Mass more than just a class. Here is a brief overview of the ingredients of our language of mystery that help us to create a climate of prayer that fosters transformation.

- **Space—**In a typical Catholic church, the stained-glass windows, the flickering votive candles, the smell of incense, a baptismal font with flowing water, statues, a large crucifix, and other sacramentals speak to us and create a climate of prayer. In our faith formation settings, we need to do likewise; the space that our learners enter should create a climate of prayer.
- **Sign and Symbol—**Standing before Michelangelo's *Pietà* or the eternal flame at the Tomb of the Unknown Soldier can bring a tear to one's eye. As a sacramental Church, we rely on signs and symbols to speak to us at a deeper level. The same should hold true for our faith formation setting. A prayer center can and should be adorned with signs and symbols that speak of the sacred. Your catechetical leader may be able to provide you with many of these sacred objects, or you may begin your own collection. You can also invite learners to bring symbols of their own to add to the prayer center.
- **Music and Singing—**Music and singing are remarkably effective at creating moods and atmosphere. Just think of how stores, shopping malls, restaurants, and other social gathering spaces use music to create a desired mood for their space. Incorporating music and song into your learning space from the moment learners enter the space can touch hearts in a way that the spoken word cannot. Today, all you need is a cell phone, a playlist, and a Bluetooth speaker to have a whole library of quality music at your fingertips.

"Fourth graders love visual aids!"

Music and the Brain

As Congresswoman Gabby Giffords was receiving therapy to recover from a gunshot wound to the head, doctors and therapists found that while she could not form words and sentences, she could sing the lyrics of songs. This is because language functions reside largely in the left side of the brain, while music functions reside not only on both sides of the brain, but also in areas deep within the brain. When we incorporate music and singing into our faith formation, we are activating the brain more extensively than through the spoken word alone.

- **Ritual—**We rely on rituals to take us out of the ordinary and into the extraordinary. Rituals have a way of invoking a mood. You can integrate numerous rituals into your faith formation sessions beginning with the ritual setting up of a prayer center, starting your session with a ritual greeting (e.g., "Our help is from the Lord," Response: "Who made heaven and earth."), and ending the session by having kids sign themselves with holy water.

> **If I should ever die, God forbid, let this be my epitaph: "The only proof he needed for the existence of God was music."**
> —Kurt Vonnegut

Ritual vs. Routine

Rituals and routines are similar with one significant difference: A routine is something we do habitually, in the same manner, and without much thought (for example, the routine we follow when we awaken each morning and get ready for work or school). A ritual, on the other hand, is something that we do habitually (on a regular basis), in the same manner, but with *deep* thought. We don't perform rituals while half-asleep. We enter into them with eyes and minds and hearts wide open, and allow them to speak to us while, at the same time, we express our deepest thoughts and beliefs.

A frustrated junior high school catechist stopped her lesson and just stood in silence in front of her noisy, misbehaving learners. Eventually, all the kids quieted down and fixed their attention on her. Finally, one of the young people asked if she was okay. The catechist replied, "My goal for this lesson was for you to be able to articulate an understanding of *conscience* and identify the *virtues*. I think now I'll just settle for thirty seconds of silence."

- **Silence and Reverence**—Few things create a mood as effectively as silence. Silence, in fact, is the most appropriate response to anything profound. We can create a climate of prayer in our learning space by incorporating periods of silence into the experience, thus teaching the virtue of reverence.
- **Gesture and Movement**—At Mass, we perform gestures and movements to both express the sacred and be reminded of the sacred. Gesture and movement reveal the connection between the physical and the spiritual. You can incorporate movements into your sessions such as a procession to enthrone the Bible and set up the prayer center. Likewise, learners can be invited to make the threefold sign of the cross on their foreheads, lips, and chests as a way of asking that God's word be in their minds, on their lips, and in their hearts.

We perform gestures and movements to both express the sacred and be reminded of the sacred.

- **Storytelling**—Stories are effective because they create moods. Ultimately, we catechists are storytellers. We are telling the story, or narrative, of our salvation, and we are inviting others to enter into that story and allow it to guide their lives. We need to remember that we are not teaching a science; rather, we are telling a profound and extraordinary story. As a catechist, you are called to share three types of stories: Scripture stories, stories of the lives of the saints, and stories of your own journey of faith and discipleship.

Let's Talk Like Catholics!

At Mass, we rely on a language of mystery to create a climate conducive to worship. For some reason, however, when it comes to faith formation, we seem to forget this language and rely exclusively on words. It's time for us to communicate like Catholics when we form others in faith, meaning that we need to include the language of mystery in our catechetical experiences if we hope to create a climate in which we facilitate encounters with the risen Christ.

Scripture

[Jesus said] 'Wherever he enters, say to the master of the house, "The Teacher says, Where is my guest room where I may eat the Passover with my disciples?" Then he will show you a large upper room furnished and ready. Make the preparations for us there.' The disciples then went off, entered the city, and found it just as he had told them; and they prepared the Passover.
MARK 14:14–16

Prayer

Jesus, before you gathered with your disciples for the Passover, you made sure all the proper preparations were taken care of. You knew that the space you were gathering in was important for what you were about to do. Help me make the arrangements I need in my learning space to make my lessons more effective and bring order and life to my lessons. May I pay great attention to the details of my sessions so that they may be as effective as possible. Amen.

Chapter Four

Assembly Instructions: The Catechetical Process

When assembling something, it is helpful to have a set of instructions so that you can follow a step-by-step process. In a similar way, catechists follow a catechetical process, which creates a rhythm and flow—a "heartbeat"—to faith formation sessions.

> **It is necessary to underline the need for a coherence between a general pedagogy of formation of catechists and the pedagogy proper to the catechetical process.**
>
> —*Directory for Catechesis*, 135d

Understanding the Catechetical Process

We mentioned earlier that St. Ignatius advised his fellow Jesuits that, when teaching, it is best to "enter through their door but be sure to leave through your door." In other words, teaching is most effective when it connects to lived experience and when it leads to a lived faith, which is to say new ways of thinking, speaking, and acting. To facilitate this movement, catechists follow what's known as a *catechetical process*.

When we gather learners to explore a theme or concept drawn from our Christian Tradition (as, for example, a particular doctrine, a story of a saint, or a Scripture passage), our efforts are most effective when we integrate the following movements, based on the work of Dr. Thomas Groome, which constitute the catechetical process:

- Name and describe an experience from the learners' world that this theme or concept speaks to.

- Invite learners to critically reflect on their present way of thinking, speaking, acting, and living in response to such experiences.
- Draw from our Catholic Tradition to shed light on the experience and to propose an alternative way for the learners to think, speak, act, and live.
- Invite learners to integrate (take ownership of) a new understanding of life inspired by our Tradition that leads to a faith response: a new way of thinking, speaking, acting, and living.

> **Jesus most often began a teaching event by inviting people to look at their present lives.**
> —Dr. Thomas Groome

Typically, faith formation presents our doctrine and theology in a systematic or linear manner. The problem with this approach is that people's lives do not unfold systematically; thus learners are often not predisposed to receive the teaching that is being offered. This systematic approach assumes that everyone is on the same page and is moving at the same speed, which does not take into account the uniqueness of individuals or families. It's like a doctor writing a prescription for the same medication for a whole group of people without giving each individual a checkup and diagnosis.

The catechetical process, on the other hand, respects the uniqueness of learners and families by making solid connections to their present lived experiences. The curriculum-driven approach delivers content in hopes that it will benefit the learner. The catechetical process creates a dialogue between our Tradition and the present lived experience of learners, leading to a new way of being human that can best be summarized as living in the *imago Dei* (the image of God). Every faith formation session we lead as catechists should have at its core the goals of delivering the content

"I'm new teaching your age group. How much do you know about systematic theology?"

Making Things Bite-Size

Experts agree that during a presentation the average person's attention is lost after ten to fifteen minutes. For catechists, the notion of "chunking," or breaking up a lesson into smaller pieces or shorter segments (which is what happens in the catechetical process), is an effective way of keeping learners engaged.

and, perhaps even more important, inspiring a transformation of hearts and minds. Let's take a closer look at the catechetical process for a typical faith formation session, following the Engage, Explore, Reflect, and Respond steps that we identified in the chapter 2.

Every faith formation session we lead as catechists should have at its core the goals of delivering the content and, perhaps even more important, inspiring a transformation of hearts and minds.

The Engage Step (ten to fifteen minutes)

In the previous chapter, we talked about preliminaries that help to establish an appropriate climate for the faith formation experience. Now, it's time to venture into your actual lesson, beginning with the **Engage** step of your session during which you seek to capture the imaginations of your learners and introduce the focus for the session. The goal of this step is to hook your learners with an image or idea from their lived experience—something they can relate to—that is also associated with the session topic or theme. Here's how it might flow:

- Introduce (announce clearly and write on the board or easel) the Big Idea.
- Invite learners to enter an icebreaker activity that enables you to "enter through their door" (i.e., draw from their lived experience, current events, popular culture, and so on) and grab their attention so that you can launch them in the direction you wish to go. Check out the example "Whom Do You Trust?" in the side bar.

Whom Do You Trust?

I once taught an eighth-grade lesson with the theme "We Trust in God Our Father." I began the Engage step by inviting the young people to print the name or initials of the person or persons they trust and then invited them to share with the group. Most referred to a best friend, a sibling, or one or both of their parents. One young man, however, very calmly stated, "No one. I don't trust anyone." I thanked him for being so honest and explained that trusting others can indeed be very difficult, especially if one's trust has been betrayed or violated. We then engaged in a very fruitful group discussion about experiences where trust had been broken. This enabled me to present God as Someone different. God is Someone who *can* be trusted because he has never broken our trust. He has kept his promises throughout the ages, culminating in the sending of his only Son, Jesus.

- Your catechist manual or leader guide often has ideas and suggestions for ways to introduce the lesson theme and engage learners. Be sure to select an idea that is age-appropriate. Don't shy away from games or icebreakers that make a point or teach a lesson related to your topic.
- To segue from the Engage step to the Explore step, invite learners to join in a moment of prayer or a few moments of silence to prepare to hear God speak to them through our Tradition.

The Explore Step (twenty-five to thirty-five minutes)

Having gotten your learners engaged, it's time to invite them to **Explore** the content of our faith Tradition that proposes an alternative way of being human. This will be the longest segment of your overall session.

- Conduct a brief review of your previous session, highlighting the Big Idea, key concepts, and vocabulary that learners can build on.
- Ground your Big Idea in Scripture by inviting a learner to come forward to read a Scripture passage that sheds light on the session theme (most catechist manuals and leader guides identify Scripture passages related to the session theme).

- Invite learners to **Explore** the content of our faith either by inviting them (sometimes in advance of your session) to interact with a textbook, view and discuss a video, or work with some other resource that reveals what our Tradition teaches about the particular topic or theme being explored.
- If reading from a textbook, be sure to pause often throughout the reading to ask discussion questions, tell stories, and check for comprehension of key words and ideas.
- Again, if reading from a textbook, consider showing a brief video that reinforces or sheds light on the content just read. Today, some faith formation programs (such as *Finding God* and *Christ Our Life* from Loyola Press) include integrated media (videos, spoken word recordings, and music accessed via QR codes) in the children's book and the catechist manual to reinforce and enliven the content.

If reading from a textbook, be sure to pause often throughout the reading to ask discussion questions, tell stories, and check for comprehension of key words and ideas.

- Engage learners in a discussion or some other activity (for example, a review game, worksheet, craft idea, role play, or learning stations) that further clarifies, fleshes out, or reinforces the content and the Big Idea. For suggestions of various activities, see chapter 5.
- Consider concluding the **Explore** step by inviting learners to listen to or sing a song, either liturgical or contemporary, that organically reinforces the theme of the session and the Big Idea.

Spoon feeding in the long run teaches us nothing but the shape of the spoon.
—E. M. Forster

The Reflect Step (ten minutes)

The most intimate step of the catechetical process is the moment we invite learners to encounter, in a very real way, the risen Christ who is in our midst. The **Reflect** step holds the key to differentiating between teaching a subject and facilitating an encounter. This step reminds us that Jesus Christ is not a subject to be taught and learned but a living Person, and that the goal of catechesis is to be in "communion and intimacy" with him (*Directory for Catechesis*, 75). The **Reflect** step is an intimate moment with Jesus. Consider the following for the **Reflect** step:

The Reflect step is an intimate moment with Jesus.

- Invite learners to transition into a very sacred time. Consider providing each learner with a small flameless tea light candle and invite them to get comfortable in their sacred space—a place in the room where they will remain during the guided reflection, which may be on the floor but in a seated position; no lying down.
- Lead a guided reflection following these steps:
  - Invite deep breathing for thirty to sixty seconds.
  - Play reflective instrumental music quietly in the background (total silence is often too jarring for young people).
  - Dim the lights if that can be done appropriately.
  - Invite learners to use their imaginations and engage all their senses in the experience (sight, sound, smell, taste, touch) as you lead them into an encounter and conversation with Jesus. St. Ignatius said that such conversation should resemble the way "one friend speaks to another" (*The Spiritual Exercises of Saint Ignatius*, 54).
  - As you lead the reflection, speak slowly and pause often to allow for silent reflection and silent conversation with Jesus.

Silence Is Golden

Research reveals that silence stimulates new cell growth in the brain, reduces tension, and improves memory. Including silence in the **Reflect** step of your session is a gift that will help your learners connect with themselves and with God.

- At the end of the guided reflection, gradually fade the instrumental music and allow a few moments of silence for learners to rest in God's presence or to continue their conversation with him.
- After an appropriate amount of time, offer a few gentle words to help learners transition back to the large group and the next activity. Invite them to open their eyes, sit up, stretch, and slowly and quietly return to their places.
- You can invite those who wish to share their experience to do so; however, demonstrate respect for their privacy by not requiring or expecting everyone to share. Another option is to invite learners to privately journal about their experience (and such entries should remain private).

Example of a Guided Reflection

Scan this QR code to listen to an example of a guided reflection.

How Long Should a Guided Reflection Be?

A good rule of thumb is to spend one minute for every year of the learners' approximate age. This translates roughly to the following:

- pre/K: three to five minutes
- primary grades: six to eight minutes
- intermediate grades: nine to eleven minutes
- junior high: twelve to thirteen minutes
- high school: fourteen to eighteen minutes

For adults, it is best to keep guided reflections in the fifteen- to twenty-minute range; anything longer can be challenging no matter how old you are.

A catechist led a guided reflection for a group of young people, and when it ended, she heard one young person whisper, "May the will of God be done." The catechist said confidently, "The will of God is always done, even without asking." The young person asked, "How can you be so sure?" The catechist responded, "I know it's true because, if it were not, there would be at least a few times when *my* will is done!"

The Respond Step (ten minutes)

Remember how we talked about St. Ignatius's advice to "enter through their door but be sure to leave through your door?" The leaving through your door time has now arrived. In this step, you will send your learners through your door and back into the world with a new set of eyes—a new way of looking at life and a new way of being human. These last few minutes of a session are an opportunity for you to review and summarize, assess how well your learners have grasped the Big Idea, invite your learners to practice a new behavior (a new way of thinking, speaking, acting) in the coming week, and finally, send your learners forth with a prayerful attitude.

- Consider using resources from your textbook or elsewhere to assess the comprehension of concepts that were presented and identify ways to apply the lesson to everyday life. We'll talk more about assessment in chapter 16.
- Consider giving an assignment that invites or challenges the learners to put into practice what has been learned and to share with others, especially their family. (Invite learners to share how they put last week's lesson into practice.)
- Lead a brief closing prayer:
  - Pause for ten to fifteen seconds of silence.
  - Pray the sign of the cross.
  - Lead learners in either a traditional prayer, a decade of the Rosary, a sung refrain, or a Mass part (Confiteor; Gloria; Creed; Holy, Holy; Lamb of God).
  - Invite learners to share a sign of peace with one another.
  - Pray the sign of the cross.

- Have learners bless themselves with holy water as they depart.
- Return the room to its usual arrangement.

By following a catechetical process, you will be doing much more than just delivering content. You will be engaging those you teach, connecting with their lived experience, accompanying them on their journey, inviting them to encounter the risen Christ who is in our midst, and equipping them with new ways of thinking, speaking, and acting as disciples of Jesus Christ. And you will be growing as a catechist!

Scripture

Now that very day two of them were going to a village seven miles from Jerusalem called Emmaus, and they were conversing about all the things that had occurred. And it happened that while they were conversing and debating, Jesus himself drew near and walked with them, but their eyes were prevented from recognizing him. He asked them, "What are you discussing as you walk along?" They stopped, looking downcast. One of them, named Cleopas, said to him in reply, "Are you the only visitor to Jerusalem who does not know of the things that have taken place there in these days?" And he replied to them, "What sort of things?" LUKE 24:13–19

Prayer

Risen Lord, as you walked the road to Emmaus with two of your disciples, you modeled for us how to follow a catechetical process and engage your followers where they were. You invited them to share their experience and to open up about the despair they were feeling. After listening to them, you gave them instruction and set their hearts on fire. The lesson, however, was not over. You broke bread with them and opened their eyes so they could recognize your presence in their midst. Help us model your example as we accompany those we teach, listen to them, reflect with them, instruct them, and invite them to encounter you and your transforming grace. Amen.

Chapter Five

Socket and Wrench Set: Finding Activities That Fit

When assembling or repairing anything with nuts and bolts, it helps to have a vast array of sockets on hand. When you find one that fits perfectly, you can get the job done. As catechists, it is imperative to choose activities that fit and help you get the job done.

> **It is therefore reasonable to offer pathways of catechesis that vary based on the learner's needs, age, and state of life.**
>
> —*Directory for Catechesis*, 225

Planning Activities That Fit

As we pointed out earlier, one of the characteristics of twenty-first century learners is that they are accustomed to switching tasks frequently. As a catechist, this means that you need an action plan that may or may not include the following: lecture, role-play, debate, creating digital presentations, gamified learning, group work, discussion, video, a guest speaker, reading text, an online review game, and so on. Like finding the right size socket, you need to determine if the activities you have chosen are the right fit both for your session theme and for your particular group of learners.

"In my opinion, he needs to use fewer parables and more scripture!"

Catechists rely on a variety of activities not only to keep learners engaged but also to ensure that the learning outcomes for the session will be achieved. Likewise, it is imperative that the activities you select are most appropriate and effective for the age group you are working with. For example, while viewing scenes from the movie *The Passion of the Christ* may be appropriate for some adult learners, it would certainly not be appropriate for young children.

Let's Get to the Bottom of This

As catechists, one of our greatest fears is that we will see bored-looking faces among our learners. The last thing we want is for faith formation experiences to be boring. Unfortunately, this is too often the perception, especially in the minds of children. But what is the cause of this boredom? Could it be the *message* that is boring? *No!* The Good News of Jesus Christ is life-changing and dramatic. It is literally a life-and-death (and life) story that contains the power to transform hearts and minds. Could it be the *messenger* that is boring? *No!* You are not boring! Human beings are not boring. Each of us is a complex being with layers and layers of experiences, dreams, fears, hopes, longings, and stories. Could it be the *method* we are using that is boring? *Bingo!* Too often the method we rely on for faith formation is boring. We either fall into the read-discuss-read-discuss trap, or we simply lecture on and on as though our learners were sponges whose job it is to soak up everything we say. These methods leave much to be desired, and the proclamation of the word of God deserves so much more.

The last thing we want is for faith formation experiences to be boring.

In this chapter, we are going to explore how to break out of these methodological ruts. We will also identify how to implement a variety of activities that will serve to unleash the energy and power of the word of God and engage the hearts and minds of learners. Our goal is to invite them to grow in their faith and live as disciples of Christ actively and intentionally.

- **Review Your Learning Outcomes—**If you are clear about your learning outcomes, you will have a good idea of the types of activities you should choose. If the learning outcomes call for the learners to articulate an understanding of a certain topic, then you need to be sure that you are not doing all of the talking! If the lesson calls for an understanding of community, it should be obvious that some type of group work would be appropriate. Common sense will often dictate which vehicle you choose.

- **Review the Age, Gender, and Spiritual Maturity of Your Group–** Visualize your group and imagine yourself executing the lesson you've planned. Ask yourself if the learners are capable of being engaged with the approach you have in mind. Perhaps they are not mature enough. On the other hand, maybe they are more sophisticated than the activity you've chosen. See the next chapter for more about the characteristics of various age groups.
- **Consult a List of Possible Learning Activities–**If you have 150 sockets in your tool kit, you'll most likely find one that fits the job at hand. As a catechist, you also have a wide range and variety of activities to select from, in addition to the activities suggested in your catechist manual or leader guide. Don't get caught in a rut of doing the same thing every time you teach. Let's delve into a list of various learning activities that you can incorporate into your lessons. Keep in mind that many of the following activities enable you to incorporate the Four Cs of twenty-first century learning: collaboration, communication, creativity, and critical thinking.

Don't get caught in a rut of doing the same thing every time you teach.

- **Speaking and Singing–**The spoken or sung word allows learners not only to learn concepts but also to express themselves and articulate and celebrate their faith while growing in the skill of social interaction and collaboration. Consider different ways you can use the following:
  - giving an elevator pitch
  - guest speakers
  - interviews
  - large-group discussions
  - lectures
  - live video guests
  - online discussions
  - panel discussions
  - playing music and songs using a smartphone paired to a Bluetooth speaker
  - podcasts
  - questions and answers
  - reading aloud to learners
  - singing (rounds, hymns, Mass parts, nursery rhymes, folk melodies)
  - small-group discussions
  - storytelling

- **The Written Word—**Some learners are more comfortable with the written word than with the spoken word. Writing is a powerful vehicle for self-discovery, prayer, and communication. Many of the saints used writing to speak with God and with others, and to record their own thoughts. In writing, your learners have an opportunity to clarify their thoughts and to make visible the invisible. Consider different ways you can use the following:
  - acrostics
  - Catholic apps
  - chain notes
  - crossword puzzles
  - digital content creation
  - e-books
  - e-mails, texts, social media posts
  - essays
  - evaluate and critique web content
  - interviews
  - letters
  - litanies
  - modern parables and stories
  - news: headlines and stories
  - one-minute essays
  - online forms and polls
  - paraphrases
  - poems
  - prayers
  - riddles
  - skits
  - slogans
  - song lyrics
  - speeches
  - summaries
  - Web pages
  - worksheets

Tell me and I forget.
Teach me and I remember.
Involve me and I learn.
—Benjamin Franklin

Benefits of Varying Your Learning Activities

Varying your learning activities provides many benefits. Good learning activities will:

- encourage creative expression
- respect varied learning styles
- help learners adjust to new settings
- create a comfortable learning environment
- develop skills such as critical thinking, problem-solving, collaboration, and conflict management
- encourage interaction
- reinforce learning
- encourage communication
- build a sense of community
- keep learners engaged

- **Role-Playing and Dramatizing**—Through the dramatic stories of our faith (Scripture and the lives of the saints), your learners can grow in creativity and critical thinking skills, come to understand themselves and others, and internalize the Christian message. Jesus used simple but dramatic stories and parables to invite people to enter into relationship with the Father. Consider different ways of using the following:
    - charades
    - choral readings
    - dance
    - dramatic readings
    - gestures to songs
    - literature
    - mime
    - pageants
    - plays
    - puppet shows
    - role-playing
    - storytelling
    - YouTube and other online videos

- **Playing Games**—Young people naturally create and participate in games. Games allow people of all ages to build community and collaboration, follow rules, learn about cooperation and participation (as opposed to only winning or losing), and develop mentally, physically, and socially. Games encourage the use of critical thinking skills and imagination. The goal of games in faith formation is not simply to have fun but to reinforce or further clarify the focus of your lesson. Consider different ways you can use the following:
  - bingo
  - board games
  - card games
  - charades
  - drawing games
  - games to find hidden objects or images
  - gamified learning
  - icebreakers
  - online simulation games
  - relays
  - skill games
  - team competitions
  - television quiz shows
  - tic-tac-toe
  - trivia games

My philosophy?
Simplicity plus variety.
—Hank Stram

The Games People Play

Studies reveal that when playing games, the motivation, attention, and participation of learners increase. Game playing can help learners embrace concepts and information that they might otherwise resist. As a catechist, take advantage of game playing to raise the level of engagement with your learners.

- **Drawing and Art**—Faith goes beyond words. Many learners express their faith through art and drawing. Your learners can grow in creativity and communication skills as they grow spiritually by visually expressing their inner thoughts and feelings. Drawing and art can also help them become more familiar with religious concepts and relate them to their own lives. Consider different ways you can use the following:
  - banners
  - booklets
  - bookmarks
  - bulletin boards
  - bumper stickers
  - buttons
  - cartoons
  - coats of arms
  - collaborative drawing
  - collages
  - comic books
  - commemorative stamps
  - dioramas
  - displays
  - doorknob hangers
  - drawing pictures and/or writing Scripture passages or quotes from saints on objects (seashells, driftwood, rocks, T-shirts)
  - finger paintings
  - flyers
  - greeting cards
  - holy cards
  - mobiles
  - modeling clay
  - mosaics
  - multimedia presentations
  - murals
  - pennants
  - photo albums
  - photo essays
  - placemats
  - plaques
  - portraits
  - posters
  - sculptures
  - sidewalk art with chalk
  - sponge paintings
  - stained glass
  - stickers
  - storybooks
  - virtual tours/field trips
  - yarn-and-cloth pictures

- **Audiovisuals**—Although some learners think and learn primarily through words, others do so through pictures, images, and sounds. People who are aural or visual learners can develop a deeper appreciation of the message in each lesson when their aural and visual imagination is engaged. Consider different ways you can use the following:
  - bulletin boards
  - chalkboards
  - charts
  - colored chalk
  - computers
  - connected classrooms
  - creating and showcasing digital content
  - digital learning stations
  - digital media
  - manipulatives
  - maps
  - models
  - online mind maps
  - pictures
  - PowerPoint presentations
  - QR codes
  - recordings
  - scrapbooks
  - slides
  - interactive whiteboards such as SMART Boards
  - tablets or smartphones
  - videos
  - virtual guest speaker
  - virtual manipulatives

Example of Integrated Multimedia

Scan this QR code to view an example of how faith formation curriculum programs such as *Finding God* and *Christ Our Life* (Loyola Press) integrate multimedia throughout the children's books and catechist/teacher guides.

Integrated Multimedia Content

We've described the needs of the twenty-first-century learner, especially the need to change tasks frequently and interact with multimedia. Some faith formation curriculum programs brilliantly integrate multimedia directly into the children's books and catechist manuals through the use of QR codes. By scanning a QR code with their phone or tablet, learners and catechists can access the following:

- **Video**—a variety of brief videos that bring to life Scripture stories and stories of the lives of the saints, which are especially beneficial to visual learners
- **Audio**—excerpts from Scripture, the *Catechism of the Catholic Church*, and other catechetical texts make our Tradition accessible, especially for auditory learners
- **Interactives**—an assortment of developmentally appropriate interactives to foster cognitive and emotional connections that also reinforce content and make learning fun
- **Text**—study guides, at-home editions, and other useful family resources

Miller's Law and Memorization

A concept known as Miller's Law (also known as the "seven plus two rule" or the "magic number seven") holds that the average person can only hold about seven (plus or minus two) ideas in their memory at a time. For catechists, this means remembering to present information that is to be memorized in small chunks that are easily digestible and retainable. For example, when teaching children to memorize the Hail Mary prayer or the Act of Contrition, it is helpful to have them memorize the prayer in smaller sections until they can put all the pieces together and recall the entire prayer from memory.

- **Memorizing, or Learning by Heart**—Through catechesis, we sustain the memory of the Church. When God gave the Israelites the Ten Commandments, he told them, "Take to heart these words which I command you today" (Deuteronomy 6:6). In faith formation, it is beneficial to learn by heart commonly known prayers and certain doctrinal formulas. Examples include the following:
    - Act of Contrition
    - Angelus
    - Apostles' Creed
    - Beatitudes
    - Corporal and Spiritual Works of Mercy
    - Deadly Sins
    - Fruit of the Spirit
    - Gifts of the Spirit
    - Glory Be
    - Grace before meals
    - Guardian Angel Prayer
    - Hail, Holy Queen
    - Hail Mary
    - Lord's Prayer
    - Mass Prayers and Responses
    - The Memorare
    - Morning Offering
    - Mysteries of the Rosary
    - Sacraments
    - Ten Commandments
    - Virtues

One day, a mother asked her very young daughter what she learned in faith formation. The daughter answered, "We learned that Jesus told us not to be scared and we'll get our quilt." Needless to say, the mom was confused. The next day, she bumped into her daughter's catechist and asked what the lesson was about. The catechist said, "Be not afraid, thy comforter is coming."

- **Select an Appropriate Activity and See If It Fits—**Once you select an activity to use, add it into your lesson plan and see if it connects with your introduction and conclusion. Ask yourself if this activity is the best vehicle to help your learners achieve the learning outcomes you have set for them. Likewise, ask yourself how this activity will help you to observe and assess those desired outcomes. If you plan to use a particular activity, be sure you are prepared with all the materials you will need.
- **Select an Alternate Activity—**Be prepared to switch gears if necessary. If your selected activity is failing, be prepared with a backup. A good example of this is the catechist who is all set to show a video only to discover that the technology is unavailable or isn't working. Always be ready to move on to an alternate plan of action.

Don't Be Afraid to Keep It Simple

While it is good to have variety in your methodology, do not lose sight of the fact that sometimes "basic white and off-white" are all you need. Often in catechesis, the simple activities of reading a text, leading a discussion, or giving a lecture actually may be the most effective strategy for a particular lesson.

Uncovering Learning

Employing a variety of activities in your lessons requires more preparation but results in more effective catechesis, a more relaxed catechist, more highly engaged learners, better discipline, and increased spontaneity on your part. Learning activities are not designed to cover material but to uncover learning!

Learning activities are not designed to cover material but to uncover learning!

Scripture

All these things Jesus spoke to the crowds in parables. He spoke to them only in parables, to fulfill what had been said through the prophet: "I will open my mouth in parables, I will announce what has lain hidden from the foundation [of the world]." MATTHEW 13:34–35

Prayer

Jesus, sometimes you told stories, other times you performed miracles. Sometimes you spoke for long stretches, other times you said very little. Sometimes you used images and metaphors, other times you spoke quite directly. You always seemed to know the right thing to say at just the right time. Help me choose the best way to bring your word to life for those I teach so that glory may be given to your name. Amen.

Chapter Six
Different Types of Wood: Adapting to Learning Styles, Disabilities, and Diversity

Some types of wood are classified as soft and others as hard, meaning that they can't all be used or handled in the same way. Similarly, the various learning styles preferred by your learners will require you to adapt and customize.

It is indispensable to respect anthropological-developmental and theological-pastoral realities, taking into account the educational sciences.

—*Directory for Catechesis*, 225

Adapt, Adapt, Adapt!

In preparing a lesson for high school students on sexuality and media, I compiled a number of clips from prime-time network TV shows and commercials that had sexual overtones. The lesson was very effective as I challenged my students to be critical of the messages they were receiving about sexuality from popular media. A parish catechetical leader then invited me to speak on a similar topic to junior high students at his parish, so I figured I would do the same learning activity with them. It was probably the most disastrous moment in my career as a catechist. I had not considered the difference between junior high and high school students. My audience of ten- to twelve-year-olds was far too immature to handle the subject matter. I had failed to adapt my lesson to the audience.

Our best response to the mission that God has entrusted to us is to gain a better understanding of the people we serve.

—John E. Barone and Charleen Katra

A Better Understanding of the People We Serve

In their excellent book *The Adaptive Teacher*, educational experts John E. Barone and Charleen Katra explain, "As catechists, educators, parish leaders, or parents, our best response to the mission that God has entrusted to us is to gain a better understanding of the people we serve. When we become more knowledgeable and sensitive to the experiences of others, we will find our own hearts responsive and magnified in turn." While Barone and Katra write specifically for those who are instructing people with disabilities, they emphasize that the adaptations they recommend can be applied to all learning differences. In this chapter, we explore the rich diversity of learning styles, the unique needs of various learners, and how you, as a catechist, can plan, lead, accompany, and respond most effectively.

- **Various Age Groups—**As mentioned in chapter 3, it is crucial to know the characteristics and learning styles of the age group you teach. You most certainly want to avoid the disaster that I described above by taking into consideration the unique characteristics and needs of the age group you teach.

Activities for Various Age Groups

Scan this QR code to view a brief video of Joe identifying examples of the kinds of learning activities that work best with various age groups.

- **Multiple Intelligences—** The concept of multiple intelligences was developed in 1983 by Dr. Howard Gardner, a professor of education at Harvard University, whose theory classifies learners according to their particular strengths. The following listing is adapted

Armed to the teeth, Sunday school teacher Nat Willowby prepares to do battle with the forces of darkness.

For weeks, a little boy was telling his kindergarten religious education class about the baby sister who was going to be coming to his house soon. One day at home, the boy's mother let him feel the baby kicking. The boy didn't say anything, and he stopped talking about the baby at religious education class. Finally, the catechist asked the boy, "Whatever happened to your new baby sister you were always talking about?" The boy burst into tears and said, "I think my mommy ate her!"

from the *Multiple Intelligences SmartCard* (Kagan Publishing and Professional Development):

- **Learning through Words**—For those who learn primarily through words (writing, reading, and discussion), be sure to invite them to brainstorm ideas, to quiz partners on vocabulary words and the spelling of words, or to summarize the contents of a session in a single word or phrase or by creating a mnemonic device.
- **Learning through Music**—For those with a good sense of rhythm and melody, be sure to integrate music into your sessions. In addition to sacred music, look for themes and issues in popular songs that are relevant to your session (caution: always be sure to preview songs for inappropriate lyrics).

Be sure to integrate music into your sessions.

- **Learning through Logic and Math**—For those who are most comfortable with numbers and patterns, be sure to invite them to connect or relate new learning to previous learning. Likewise, create word problems or play questioning games, such as Twenty Questions, which involves the recognition of patterns.
- **Learning through Art and Space**—For those who prefer to express themselves through art, be sure to offer opportunities to summarize session themes by making posters, collages, graphs, or charts. Likewise, consider experiences of *visio divina* ("divine seeing") in which we invite God to speak to our hearts as we look upon an image of sacred art (such as the *Finding God* Art Prints by Loyola Press).

Art and Faith

Research shows that art is important for learners, especially for young children. Studies reveal that art activities increase brain capacity by engaging children's senses. For centuries, the Church has relied on sacred art to invite learners to encounter the divine. As a catechist, you can tap into this tradition by including activities that encourage learning through art.

- **Learning through Physical Activity**—For those who learn best when they are invited to *do* something (*haptic* learners) be sure to include gestures, body language, and hands-on activities. Consider using role-playing, athletic activities, simulation exercises, ASL (American Sign Language), and content-based games, such as charades and pantomimes, which involve physical movement and tactile activity.
- **Learning through Nature**—For those who learn best when the content of a lesson is related to nature, consider conducting outdoor scavenger hunts, or invite them to create observation notebooks in which they record how they see God's presence in the world around them. Don't hesitate to use microscopes, telescopes, or other scientific equipment in observing the complexity of creation.

> **Nature is the source of all true knowledge.**
> —Leonardo da Vinci

- **Learning through Interaction**—For those who learn best by interacting with others, be sure to provide peer activities, small-group projects and discussions, and large-group activities. You can also develop a pattern for small-group discussions that includes reporting to the larger group.
- **Learning through Introspection**—For those who learn best when given time to process information on their own, incorporate independent learning activities, self-designed study projects, and

reflective journaling. Consider learner portfolios to provide introspective learners an opportunity to express themselves in ways they are most comfortable.

Paying Attention to Those with Disabilities—You can do much to enhance and emphasize the unity of the Body of Christ by incorporating a positive recognition of the differences in individual abilities. When working with anyone who has a disability, it is important to communicate with your catechetical leader or principal for assistance. Likewise, just as it is important to learn the language of catechesis, it is important to learn and use appropriate terminology when referring to a learner's disability. Here is an overview of some of the disabilities that learners in your group may have, as well as suggestions for helping them.

Just as it is important to learn the language of catechesis, it is important to learn and use appropriate terminology when referring to a learner's disability.

- **Orthopedic Impairment**—Adapt activities to fit the needs of learners who are physically challenged, encourage social interaction, and provide assistance such as a buddy system.
- **Visual Impairment**—For those with visual impairments, provide large-print, audio, and manual materials, and consider range of vision as well as lighting needs when arranging where the individual will be seated. Include activities that rely on senses other than sight, and allow visually impaired learners to work orally; invite another learner to function as his or her partner for activities that are highly visual.
- **Deafness or Hearing Impairment**—Arrange for learners with hearing impairments to be seated near the front of the room, face the individual when you speak, and speak clearly. Write key words and directions on the board in addition to providing written materials, turn on subtitles for videos, and encourage social interaction. If

A picture is worth a thousand words. Let your learners draw pictures; a picture is a lot easier to give feedback on than a thousand-word essay!

needed and in cooperation with the individual's family and your catechetical leader, arrange for an interpreter.

- **Speech or Language Impairment—**Speak clearly and in short phrases, use visual and written instructions, and allow extra time for those with a language barrier or speech impairment to respond to questions and comments. If needed, arrange for an aide to work with the learner.
- **Social or Behavioral Problems, Attention Disorders, and Learning Disabilities—**Work with the family and your catechetical leader to identify the learner's needs and make adaptations to enable the individual to experience success. Consider the following: arrange the room to avoid distractions; provide structure and routine; give specific tasks that are interesting to the learner; give, review, and clarify directions, expectations, and explanations; frequently monitor and affirm appropriate behavior; provide immediate feedback; develop nonverbal clues for unacceptable behavior; break down tasks into smaller, less overwhelming components; use flash cards when appropriate; introduce skills one at a time; rely on visual aids and movement or gestural cues; and request an aide for individualized attention when needed.
- **Mental Impairment—**Adapt activities to the learner's attention span and levels of coordination and skill. Individualize learning with the help of an aide, simplify concepts, and repeat your statements periodically. Arrange for another learner to partner with the individual to help when needed.

True story: A parish catechetical leader and her catechists were rehearsing with children preparing to receive their First Holy Communion. One of the children with special needs was completely uninhibited in showing his joy and excitement while practicing their procession up the aisle. The catechists gently tried to persuade the boy to show more reverence and to refrain from dancing and cheering as he walked toward the sanctuary. Finally, the catechetical leader said to her catechists, "You know what? Let's leave him be. He's actually the one who's got it right! We should *all* be dancing and cheering as we approach the Eucharist!"

Giftedness: Challenge gifted and talented learners through independent study, small-group work, enrichment activities, and discovery learning related to their interests. Strive to provide supplementary resources. Use creative puzzles and games. Ask gifted and talented individuals to help with preparing chapter materials and with assisting slower or younger learners. Encourage high-level thinking skills.

For more information about skills, strategies, and tips for working with those who have disabilities, contact the National Catholic Partnership on Disability (NCPD) at ncpd.org.

Cultural Inclusivity—When it comes to the Body of Christ, St. Paul said, "As a body is one though it has many parts, and all the parts of the body, though many, are one body, so also Christ" (1 Corinthians 12:12). Diversity is a hallmark of the Body of Christ. Here are some tips for practicing cultural inclusivity:

- Be aware of the diversity in your group and do your homework about traditions, customs, and values of the various ethnic groups present in your group. Invite learners to share their own unique customs and traditions.

Diversity is a hallmark of the Body of Christ.

- Cultural sensitivity goes beyond ethnicity to include awareness that many learners come from families experiencing divorce, are members of mixed families, or even have experienced various forms of abuse.
- Learners may also come from families that do not often attend Sunday Mass and may not be familiar with church traditions or practices.
- Visually reflect the diversity of your group through the display of posters, pictures, and figures of Jesus, the saints, and Bible characters that were created by the cultures of your group.
- Be sure your sessions reflect the diversity in your group, including various prayer styles and devotions that are customary in certain ethnic groups.

¿Hablas español?

Experts predict that by the year 2050, two-thirds of all U.S. Catholics will be Hispanic. Now might be a good time to learn some Spanish if you haven't already!

- Guard against materials, images, and situations that stereotype people of certain ethnic backgrounds. Likewise, avoid qualifiers that reinforce stereotypes (for example, identifying someone as "that articulate Black man," thus suggesting that he is the exception to the rule, or "I don't see color," which suggests that you can see past their "shortcoming").
- Identify people by race or ethnic origin only when it is relevant. In other words, if it is inappropriate to say, "Cardinal So-and-So, our white archbishop," then it is also inappropriate to say, "Bishop So-and-So, our Hispanic auxiliary bishop."
- Be aware of language that, to some people, has questionable racial or ethnic connotations (for example, people of color who survived a hurricane being referred to as "refugees").
- Be aware of the possible negative implications of color-symbolic words and phrases and ethnic-symbolic words and phrases (for example, "someone with a black reputation" or "Indian giver").
- Avoid tokenism toward any racial or ethnic group. In other words, be inclusive consistently, not just with a once-per-year gesture (for example, once a year, in honor of Martin Luther King Day, we'll look at a Black saint).

Compare Notes

One of the most helpful things that you can do as a catechist is to compare notes with fellow catechists who are, as they say, in the same boat as you. Parish catechetical leaders often form grade-level or age-level groupings of catechists and encourage them to meet to share tips and strategies for working with that group. Likewise, catechists who work with people with disabilities can greatly benefit by comparing notes with other catechists in the same ministry. Today, the benefits of social media and technology make it easy for you to connect with other catechists to compare notes and share strategies for more effectively meeting the unique needs of your learners.

Scripture

To the Jews I became like a Jew to win over Jews; to those under the law I became like one under the law—though I myself am not under the law—to win over those under the law. To those outside the law I became like one outside the law—though I am not outside God's law but within the law of Christ—to win over those outside the law. To the weak I became weak, to win over the weak. I have become all things to all, to save at least some. All this I do for the sake of the gospel, so that I too may have a share in it.
1 Corinthians 9:20–23

Prayer

St. Paul taught us that, for the sake of the gospel, we should strive to become "all things to all." Holy Spirit, help me recognize the wide variety of gifts that are present in the group I teach. Help me recognize the special needs that some individuals have, and then help me make the necessary adjustments to meet the needs of all my learners. Help me become all things to all people so that I might build up the Body of Christ. Amen.

Chapter Seven

Spotlights: Shifting the Focus onto Learners

> **At the appropriate time, the companion [catechist] is capable of stepping aside, thus fostering in the learners a first-person assumption of responsibility for their own journey of faith.**
>
> —*Directory for Catechesis*, 263

Repairs being done in dark, dingy spaces require a spotlight, which too often gets turned around and shines on us instead of on what we're repairing. In faith formation, the spotlight of attention is not supposed to be directed at the catechist but rather on those we teach.

Putting the Focus on Your Learners, Not on Yourself

When I was a student teacher, I was very proud of the first class I taught. My mouth had a motor on it, and I never ran out of gas. When class was over, my cooperating teacher congratulated me on surviving and said that I did a good job. Then, he bluntly said, "Problem is, you talk too much." I said, "I thought teachers were supposed to talk." "Yes," he replied, "but not all the time. The spotlight is not supposed to be on you, it's supposed to be on your students. They are the ones who are supposed to perform, not you."

This was a "Copernican Revolution" for me, but it made great sense. If I do all the performing, then I become an entertainer, and the learners become a passive audience. In every learning space, there is a spotlight waiting to shine. Our goal as catechists is to turn that spotlight around and shine it on our learners. When we shift the focus from ourselves onto our apprentices, it allows us to see the extent to which they are learning to think, speak, and act differently.

Our goal as catechists is to turn that spotlight around and shine it on our learners.

A Copernican Revolution

Nicolaus Copernicus was a Polish astronomer credited with proposing the theory that the sun, not the earth, is the center of the solar system. We use the term "Copernican Revolution" to refer to an individual who comes to the realization that he or she is not the center of the universe or, as in this case, the center of attention. This realization is extremely helpful to catechists because it takes pressure off us to perform instead of facilitating the performance of our learners.

Gone are the days when the catechist's job was primarily to impart information. In today's world, learners can acquire information from a variety of sources right at their fingertips. This in no way makes the role of the catechist obsolete. Quite the contrary. The twenty-first century catechist can focus much more on serving as a facilitator of encounters with the risen Christ as opposed to being the font of all knowledge. It also means that we no longer look at learners as sponges who simply soak up the knowledge being imparted to them but rather as fellow pilgrims that we accompany; pilgrims who share in the responsibility of "taking the oars" on this spiritual journey aboard the Barque of St. Peter, the Church.

The Catechist as Facilitator

To facilitate means "to make easy." Just as a can of oil is used to lubricate the joints and gears of a piece of machinery so that it runs more smoothly, a facilitator relies on certain skills and techniques to enable a group of learners to work together smoothly. Most important, to facilitate means to place yourself in the service of others, just as Jesus taught us to serve. Let's look at some of the ways that you, as a catechist, can shift the focus onto your learners so that you can concentrate on facilitating the proceedings:

> **"A person cannot teach another person directly; a person can only facilitate another's learning."**
> —Carl Rogers

- **Review Your Session Plan**—How much talking are *you* planning to do? Sometimes lecturing might be necessary; but if you are planning to do all the talking, when and how will the learners learn to express their faith? Instead of asking yourself, "How am I going to impart this knowledge to them?" ask, "How will they access this knowledge and articulate their understanding of it?"
- **Review Your Learning Outcomes**—Remember, the learning outcomes for your session are not statements about what *you* are going to do, but descriptions of what your *learners* are going to do. If your outcomes call for learners to articulate an understanding of the Beatitudes, then that means *they* are to articulate that understanding—not you. Most catechetical resources articulate the learning outcomes for a session. The key to learning outcomes is that they must be measurable: they must identify a behavior or skill that you will be able to look for (assess). The following is a convenient chart that provides some key words for measurable learning outcomes progressing through a hierarchy of six cognitive skills: remember, understand, apply, analyze, evaluate, and create (Bloom's Taxonomy).

> **Begin with the end in mind.**
> —Stephen Covey

> A wise Native American proverb expresses the following truth: "Tell me, and I'll forget. Show me, and I may not remember. Involve me, and I'll understand."

If you want your learners to . . .	**Use key words like these in your learning outcomes:**		**Example:** *After this lesson, the learners will be able to . . .*
. . . **remember** (recognize, retrieve, or recall facts, information, and knowledge)	list define fill in name	describe repeat label identify	. . . list the seven sacraments.
. . . **understand** (demonstrate comprehension by explaining ideas and concepts)	paraphrase review discuss	explain match interpret	. . . explain the meaning of the symbol of water in baptism.
. . . **apply** (connect or use what is learned in new situations)	draw sketch write	construct simulate predict	. . . draw a picture of an experience of reconciliation in their lives.
. . . **analyze** (assess and connect important points, recognize parts, structure, or relationship)	classify differentiate contrast separate	distinguish compare categorize break down	. . . categorize the seven sacraments into Sacraments of Initiation, Sacraments of Healing, and Sacraments at the Service of Communion.
. . . **evaluate** (judge and justify ideas based on standards and criteria)	judge assess decide rate argue	appraise defend debate choose	. . . consider a sample homily for a confirmation Mass in relation to its use of the gifts of the Holy Spirit, the symbols of the bishop, or the symbols of the rite of confirmation.
. . . **create** (combine concepts to form something new and original)	combine put together assemble	relate integrate collect	. . . assemble a prayer aid for the celebration of one of the seven sacraments.

- **Identify How Learners Will Be Engaged in Learning—**Learners can demonstrate learning and comprehension in many ways (as discussed in chapter 6). Don't rely solely on oral expression. Provide your learners with options (drawing, writing, role-playing, poster making, etc.) by which they can demonstrate an understanding of content. Experts tell us that learners retain a much higher percentage of what they *do*. Get your learners *doing*.

> **A goal without a plan is just a wish.**
> —Antoine de Saint-Exupéry

- **Do a Check-In—**At the beginning of a session consider doing a check-in, which enables you to take the pulse of your group and get learners in touch with their state of mind and spirit. Here are some examples of questions you can ask: "What emotion are you feeling the most today?" "What was the best part of the past week for you?" "What might get in the way of you fully participating or learning today?" "How would you describe your past week in weather terms (stormy, cloudy, foggy, mostly sunny)?" "What is bringing you the most energy in your life right now?" This strategy is especially effective with adult learners.

- **Ask Learners to Recall Important Points Covered in the Previous Session—**Learning needs to be reinforced. A good way to do that and to get your learners thinking and speaking instead of you doing all the talking is to ask them to recall important concepts covered in your previous session. Don't hesitate to give a spot quiz at the start of a session to assess their ability to recall important concepts or key words.

> **Learning needs to be reinforced.**

Can You Repeat That?

Studies done by neurophysiologists show that one of the most significant components of learning is repetition, which helps learners retain learned information. Taking a few moments to review what was covered in your previous session can help learners to retain information over the long haul.

- **Ask Your Learners to Solve the Problem**—The Good News that we teach is intended to address some form of bad news or problem we are facing. For example, if the focus of your session is on the importance of listening to voices that guide us to the truth, you might invite learners to identify voices that may not be trustworthy and should not be heeded. You can then ask them to identify voices that can and should be trusted. After they have done all this work, you can simply summarize and fill in examples they have missed.
- **Be Prepared with Open-Ended Questions**—Strive to use questions that are open-ended or, simply put, those that cannot be answered with a *yes* or *no*. For example, instead of asking, "Do you remember your first communion?" ask, "What are some of the things you remember about your first communion?" Granted, you may still get one-word answers, but if you have more than yes or no, you can at least begin making a list on the board for further discussion. (For more information about techniques for asking questions, see chapter 8.)
- **Develop Techniques for Deflecting**—Difficult questions can put the bright glare of the spotlight right on you. Learn to deflect such questions by shifting the attention away from yourself and onto the question. Respond to a difficult question by tossing it back at the questioner ("What do *you* think?") or by inviting anyone else in the group to share their thoughts while you compose yourself and collect your own thoughts. Jesus was particularly good at this. He often responded to a question with a question (e.g., Matthew 21:23-25). Don't hesitate to admit that you don't know the answer but say that you will do some research and get back to them with what you found.
- **Survey What Was Learned**—At the end of your session, invite every learner to recall and share at least one significant insight, key word, or concept from the session. Not only is this a good way to invite your learners to speak up, but it also serves as a good opportunity for you to assess their comprehension of the lesson.

"That's an interesting question, Andrea. No matter what answer I give, your parents will kill me."

A catechist began her lesson with a question: "Boys and girls, what do we know about God?" A hand shot up in the air. "He is an artist!" said a young boy. "Really?! How do you know?" the catechist asked. "You know—'Our Father, who does art in heaven . . .'"

Resist the Temptation to Be the Font of All Knowledge

I imagine it would have been easier for Jesus if he had given a lecture to his disciples about who he was. Instead, he asked them two questions: "Who do people say that I am?" and "Who do *you* say that I am?" (Mark 8:27, 29; emphasis added). Jesus did not jump in with the correct answer but waited for the disciples to offer their best responses. As catechists, we, too, need to resist the temptation to be the font of all knowledge and instead help our learners grapple with the questions of life and faith and guide them to the truth.

Make Sure the Spotlight Is Evenly Distributed

Just as you need to be sure that the spotlight is not always on you as the catechist, you need to be sure that it is being evenly distributed throughout the group. As you are pacing yourself through a session, keep an eye out to make sure that no one dominates the proceedings on one extreme, and no one is being left out on the other extreme. Keep an eye out for the following four types of learners in your group:

- **The Dominator**—the learner who talks way too much and doesn't allow space for others
- **The Shy One**—the shy person who rarely volunteers
- **The Tangent Maker**—the learner who has a habit of steering the conversation in an unhelpful direction
- **The Antagonist**—the learner who has an agenda or axe to grind

Experts tell us that learners retain a much higher percentage of what they *do* compared with what they hear or see. Get your learners *doing*.

Four Types of Learners

Scan this QR code to view a brief video of Joe sharing strategies for dealing with the four types of learners who may pose challenges in your group.

Scripture

Nothing is concealed that will not be revealed, nor secret that will not be known. What I say to you in the darkness, speak in the light; what you hear whispered, proclaim on the housetops. MATTHEW 10:26–27

Prayer

Jesus, I believe that you have spoken to my learners in the dark, mysterious corners of their hearts. Help me shine the light on them so that they will bring out what is concealed and make known what is hidden. Give me the courage and strength I need to resist the temptation to talk all the time. Help me put the focus on my learners so that they will come to realize that the real light comes from within. Amen.

Chapter Eight
Scrapers: Asking Questions to Get beneath the Surface

In our first house, the job of removing the old wallpaper in the living room proved to be no easy task. Fortunately, with my scraper and some elbow grease, I was able to get down to the beautiful natural surface that had been hidden. In faith formation, we use questions to get beneath the surface and uncover the potential of our learners.

> **Catechesis is an authentic laboratory of dialogue, because in the depths of every single person it encounters the vivacity and complexity, the desires and inquiries, the limitations and at times also the errors of the society and cultures of the contemporary world.**
>
> —*Directory for Catechesis*, 54

Getting beneath the Surface

Our learners are so full of potential. We just need to know how to get beneath the surface or exterior to unlock that potential. As catechists, one of the most effective ways we do this is by *asking questions*. Jesus was, of course, a master at this skill. Often in the Gospels, we find Jesus utilizing questions to challenge his followers and stimulate their thinking. As catechists, we too need to utilize questions in our lessons so that we may get beneath the surface of our learners and tap into the rich potential that lies inside of them.

Jesus effectively used questions as part of his teaching approach. Here are just a few examples:

- "But who do you say that I am?" (Mark 8:29)
- "Whose image is this and whose inscription?" (Matthew 22:20)
- "Which is easier, to say, 'Your sins are forgiven,' or to say, 'Rise and walk'?" (Luke 5:23)
- "Can the wedding guests fast while the bridegroom is with them?" (Mark 2:19)
- "Which of these three, in your opinion, was neighbor to the robbers' victim?" (Luke 10:36)

We imitate Jesus through the art of effective questioning in our faith formation setting.

Grappling with the Right Questions

One of Jesus's most famous sayings refers to the act of asking a question: "Ask and it will be given to you" (Matthew 7:7). I have come to believe that our task as catechists is not so much to provide answers for our learners but to teach them to grapple with the right questions. When they ask, they will receive. Let's look at some techniques for asking questions.

I have come to believe that our task as catechists is not so much to provide answers for our learners but to teach them to grapple with the right questions.

- **Plan Your Questions ahead of Time**—The Leader Guide for your catechetical resource most likely offers questions for discussion. Look these over ahead of time to make sure they will serve your purposes. Don't hesitate to prepare additional questions of your own. Write out your questions ahead of time so that you don't go blank when you need them. Shorten and rephrase them until you feel they will achieve their goal most effectively.

Phrase Your Questions in a Simple, Straightforward Way—Avoid complicated questions that turn and twist so much that learners can't figure out what you're really looking for. Keep the question short and to the point, and as mentioned earlier, keep them open-ended.

"You could read all of these books and none of them would really answer you, but by the time you'd finish, you'd have learned to live with the question."

Don't Answer Your Own Questions—All too often, catechists panic when no one volunteers to answer a question and, to save face, they answer the question themselves. Remember what we said earlier about putting the spotlight on your learners? When you ask a question, you have placed the focus—the spotlight—on the learners. Keep it there. Be patient. Give the learners time to think. If they're having trouble answering, try rephrasing the question.

Here's an example of an open-ended question. Instead of asking, "Did Jesus ever show any feelings or emotions?" you would ask, "What are some examples of times when Jesus showed his feelings or emotions?"

Ask a Question, Pause, and Then Repeat It—Asking a question once is never enough. Get in the habit of asking a question, pausing (providing wait time), and then asking the question again in the same way. Do this even if a hand shoots up after the first time. By pausing and repeating the question, you give learners who may be slower to process and respond an opportunity to jump in instead of always calling on the extroverts who react more quickly.

Asking a question once is never enough.

- **As You Await an Answer, Move around the Room and Make Eye Contact**—This is a technique to communicate that you expect an answer to the question and will wait until you get one.
- **Ask a Question of the Whole Group First**—Whenever you ask a question, direct it to the whole group because if you single out one learner, the rest of the group will think that they're off the hook. Occasionally, you may need to single out someone whose attention is flagging, but more often than not, the whole group should have the opportunity to respond.
- **Allow Learners to Use "Lifelines"**—The TV show *Who Wants to Be a Millionaire* allowed contestants to use "lifelines" if they weren't sure of an answer. Consider doing the same when an individual learner seems stumped by a question, even after you've allowed sufficient wait time. Allow the learner to "call a friend" who can help them answer the question.
- **Base Your Questions on the Learning Outcomes for Your Session**—Back in chapter 7, we talked about making sure that your learning outcomes are measurable: they must identify a behavior or skill that you will be able to observe. In other words, you need to be sure what cognitive domain you are aiming for (knowledge, understanding, application, analysis, evaluation, synthesis). Your questions should then be formulated to elicit responses at the level.
- **Give Feedback to Learners When They Respond to Questions**—If a learner answers a question and you do not acknowledge the answer, he or she may feel ignored or unappreciated. Learners participate more if they feel that their contributions are appreciated. Be sure to tell learners "That's excellent," or "You make a very good point." Even if a learner answers incorrectly, do not embarrass him or her by saying, "No, you're wrong." Instead, say something such as "Not quite, although I can see why you thought of that. Let's see if someone can help you."

> **We are closer to God when we are asking questions than when we think we have the answers.**
> —Abraham Joshua Heschel

- **Avoid Questions That Contain the Answers**—Your questions should not contain or imply the answer ("implied-response" questions). For example, a question such as "Don't we all agree that John's Gospel is very different from the Gospels of Matthew, Mark, or Luke?" tips the learners as to the response the catechist wants and does nothing to encourage them to generate their own thoughts. A better way of phrasing this question might be, "Of the four Gospels, which one stands out as being unique, and what makes it so unique compared to the others?"
- **Develop a Sequence of Questions (Scaffolding)**—Allow your questions to build on one another. In some cases, your questions might encourage learners to recall information that is best understood in sequence. For example, "We learned that the seven sacraments are arranged in three categories. Who can give me the first category?" (Sacraments of Initiation: baptism, confirmation, Eucharist). Likewise, your questions can gradually move learners from easier levels of understanding to more complex levels. Don't hesitate to ask challenging questions that invite critical thinking.
- **Avoid Affirmative Statements as Questions**—Catechists sometimes ask questions such as "Does everybody understand this?" or "Is everybody with me?" which encourages learners to simply nod their heads in affirmation, even if they don't understand. Such questions imply that you don't really want a response and that you would like to move on. A better way to ask this question might be, "What questions about ________________ do you have?" which makes it clear that you are intentionally taking a break to see if anyone needs clarification before moving on. Even better, consider asking learners to write down what is most confusing or difficult to comprehend about the content just presented and then invite them to offer their questions.
- **Make Your Questions Precise**—Learners can easily become confused if a question is vague or imprecise, such as, "What does Jesus mean here?" Instead ask, "What does Jesus mean when he tells us to turn the other cheek?"
- **Turn the Tables**—The game show *Jeopardy* is known for providing answers to which contestants must provide the questions. Consider doing the same by prompting, "If this is the answer . . . , what is the question?" For example, "If the answer is 'Matthew, Mark, Luke, and John,' what is the question?" ("What are the four Gospels?")

Research shows that people engage in conversations for two primary reasons: to access or exchange information and to bond with another person. Research also shows that asking questions achieves both goals. Asking questions (not just recall questions) of your learners unlocks learning while also communicating to your learners that you are interested in what they have to say. It is a sign of true accompaniment.

Types of Questions: The Four I's—There are four basic types of questions that enable you to scaffold or build up to higher level questioning. The four types of questions are further arranged in two categories: *impersonal* and *personal*.

Impersonal

- **Informational**—These questions skim the surface and are very nonthreatening. Asking an informational question is a great way to begin a discussion. For example, "The Beatitudes are part of a longer discourse that Jesus gave. What do we call that discourse?" The answer is strictly informational: "The Sermon on the Mount."
- **Implicational**—These questions go beneath the surface in search of significance. For example, "What is Jesus trying to tell us in the Beatitudes?" The response is beyond informational but does not require the responder to necessarily reveal anything personal.

Personal

- **Individual**—These questions delve into the thoughts, opinions, and feelings of the individual responding. For example, "How can *you* try to live out the Beatitudes in your life?" Obviously, this type of question can seem a bit more threatening because more is being revealed. On the other hand, it can lead to a more meaningful and enjoyable discussion.
- **Ideological**—These questions invite learners to speculate and to grapple with deep issues rather than to give right or wrong answers. For example, "What do you think the world would look like if everyone lived the Beatitudes?" To respond on this level is to reveal one's personal thoughts, hopes, and dreams.

The Socratic Method

Even as we move further into the twenty-first century, some ancient methods of teaching remain quite useful. One such method, known as the Socratic method, is based on an approach attributed to the great Greek philosopher Socrates (fifth century BC). Socrates was known for engaging young minds by asking questions designed to help them grapple with complex ideas. In the Socratic method, open-ended questions take precedence over the delivery of information and facts. As a result, the teacher acts more as a facilitator of a conversation rather than as a lecturer.

In the Socratic method, open-ended questions take precedence over the delivery of information and facts.

The goal of the Socratic method is to encourage and even prod learners to discover truths on their own while also grappling with arguments both for and against the topic. For example, a catechist may present a moral dilemma and invite learners to weigh in with their position and reasoning. Then, after reading or viewing materials that present the Catholic principles that apply to the dilemma, the catechist may ask if they still hold the same position considering the principles presented. The key is to involve multiple learners so that the learners are exposed to a wide range of points of view.

The Socratic method is most effective with older learners and adults, who are encouraged to explore their thoughts and beliefs, building critical thinking skills in the process. The goal is not simply to allow students to express their own opinions and arrive at their own "truths," but rather, to ask questions that invite learners to evaluate the solidity and soundness of their stance considering Catholic principles and gospel values.

Keep in mind that the Socratic method should never be used to show up, shame, or intimidate a learner by publicly exposing inconsistencies in their arguments, nor should it be used to show off one's own superior knowledge or moral standing. Rather, the method is a vehicle for exploring truth, developing analytical and oral skills, and deepening learner engagement and ownership of their own faith formation.

I cannot teach anybody anything; I can only make them think.

—Socrates

A catechist asked her learners, "Does anyone here know what we mean by sins of omission?"
A small girl replied, "Aren't those the sins we should have committed but didn't?"

Leading Discussions

Scan this QR code to view a brief video of Joe sharing more tips on leading discussions.

Leading Discussions—Asking questions in your sessions is part of the larger context of leading discussions. Discussions are an important means of assessing learners' understanding of a topic. Discussions promote active engagement in learning and allow learners an opportunity to express themselves. When leading discussions, consider the following:

- Encourage respectful listening.
- Assure confidentiality.
- Ask questions that, instead of simply inviting learners to retrieve information, invite them to share thoughts, opinions, and feelings.
- Invite more than one response to a question.
- Ask for reactions to previous responses, such as "Do you agree with what (Name) said?"
- Occasionally, summarize what you heard others say and invite more discussion.

A Positive Learning Culture

Aside from assessing comprehension, effective questioning techniques enable you to develop a positive learning culture in your faith formation setting by encouraging deeper level dialogue that results in increased understanding and learning. This benefits you as a catechist as well as your learners who are seeking to find their way in an often-confusing world. Effective questioning also contributes to the climate of prayer that we discussed earlier, reminding learners that we are grappling with mystery, not studying a science.

Scripture

Then the disciples of John approached him and said, "Why do we and the Pharisees fast [much], but your disciples do not fast?" Jesus answered them, "Can the wedding guests mourn as long as the bridegroom is with them?"
MATTHEW 9:14–15

Prayer

Jesus, you knew how to ask questions of your followers to help them come to understand the truth. Help me ask questions of my learners that will get beneath the surface and delve into their hearts. Help me unlock their true potential so that the power of your Spirit may be unleashed. Help me use questions as if I were scraping away old paint or wallpaper, revealing the true beauty of each learner in the process. Help me teach them to ask the right questions of life; thus, its mysteries will gradually be revealed to them, and they will come to recognize time and again that you are the answer they are seeking. Amen.

Chapter Nine

A Power Source: Plugging into the Power of Prayer

It's frustrating when you have all the tools you need to begin a home improvement project, but you're missing the one thing that will get you going: a connection to electricity! In faith formation, it is crucial that we plug into the power of the Holy Spirit.

Catechesis has the task of educating the believer for prayer and in prayer, developing the contemplative dimension of Christian experience.

—*Directory for Catechesis*, 86

The Power of Prayer

There is a world of difference between saying, "Let me tell you about someone" and "I'd like to introduce you to someone." The former can be compared to teaching a subject. The latter is the essence of facilitating encounters. In faith formation, prayer is the key to moving from the former to the latter.

Unfortunately, in faith formation, prayer is often relegated to a couple of perfunctory bookend moments at the beginning and end of our session: a quick Hail Mary, Our Father, or Glory Be (and why do we refer to it as a quick prayer, as if apologizing for taking up people's time?). Many catechists feel pressure to cover "the important stuff" (doctrine) and end up pushing prayer to the peripheries as if it were fluff. We need to remember that prayer, along with creed, sacraments, and morality, is one of the four pillars of the *Catechism of the Catholic Church*. Without prayer, we are basically inviting our learners to balance themselves on a three-legged chair. Without prayer, we lose our balance.

We cannot love God with our head alone. Through prayer, we learn to love God with our whole heart, soul, mind, and strength as we deepen our relationship with him. In this chapter, we're going to look at how you as a catechist can more thoroughly and effectively integrate prayer into your faith formation sessions.

We cannot love God with our head alone. Through prayer, we learn to love God with our whole heart, soul, mind, and strength.

- **Taking Traditional Prayers to Heart: Memorization and Prayer**—One of the ways that we sustain the "memory" of the Church is through the memorization, or the "taking to heart," of traditional prayers. Memorizing (taking to heart) traditional prayers is like embracing a family heirloom that has been passed from generation to generation. These prayers link your learners to ancient truths of our faith, they provide us with words to pray when we cannot find our own, and they enable groups of people to pray aloud together. Invite learners to take prayers to heart by memorizing them, to dive deeply into the meaning of the words, and to recite them together in your sessions.

- ***Lectio divina***—Latin for "divine reading," *lectio divina* is a way of spending time with the word of God (Scripture) using a prayerful form of reading and listening so that we can hear God with, as St. Benedict put it in his Prologue to the Rule, "the ear of our hearts." In our hectic world, this quiet, contemplative form of prayer is a welcome respite, allowing God's word to sink into our being. This form of prayer follows four steps:

Memorizing (taking to heart) traditional prayers is like embracing a family heirloom that has been passed from generation to generation.

  - ***Lectio*** (reading)—Invite learners to get comfortable and to quiet themselves. Slowly and prayerfully read aloud a brief Scripture passage, repeating the passage up to three times with a silent pause between each reading. After one of the readings of the passage, invite learners to share, without trying to fully explain, a word or phrase that is speaking to them.

- ***Meditatio*** (meditation)—Invite learners to silently reflect for a few minutes upon the word or phrase that is speaking to them, allowing it to interact with their own thoughts, hopes, desires, and memories.
- ***Oratio*** (responding)—For a few minutes, invite learners to enter into a silent dialogue with God, speaking as one friend speaks to another, allowing themselves to be touched and changed by God's word.
- ***Contemplatio*** (contemplation)—Invite learners to rest silently and prayerfully in God's embrace for a few minutes. By letting go of their own words, learners allow the word of God to speak to their hearts and be heard in the silence.

Learn to know the Heart of God in the Words of God.
—Pope St. Gregory the Great

Visio Divina

Like *lectio divina*, *visio divina* is a way of praying with our eyes and encountering the beauty of God who speaks to our hearts as we gaze upon a sacred image. Simply display a sacred image and invite learners to let their gaze fall prayerfully upon the image, paying attention to the shapes, colors, lighting, facial expressions, and every detail in the image. Invite learners to prayerfully reflect on the part of the image to which their attention is most drawn; ask how God is speaking to their heart through the image. Invite learners to prayerfully respond to God, and then to rest in prayerful silence, savoring the intimacy of a moment shared with God.

Seeing Is Believing

Experts estimate that over 60 percent of learners are visual, meaning that they process information that they can *see* better than information that they *hear*. *Visio divina* provides you with a vehicle for tapping into this preference typical of so many learners.

- **The Daily Examen—**The daily Examen is a brief prayer—about ten to fifteen minutes depending on the age of the group—that invites learners to conduct a review of their day so that they can recognize God's presence in the rearview mirror of life. The daily Examen can be a great way to bring closure to your faith formation experience and, as with the reflective prayer, is something you can invite them to practice on their own. Invite them to follow these simple steps:
  - **Ask God for Light—**pray for the grace to look at their day with God's eyes.
  - **Give Thanks—**recognize that their day is a gift from God.
  - **Prayerfully Review the Day—**look back, with the guidance of the Holy Spirit, on the day just completed to see where they can recognize God and how they have responded by either moving closer to him or away from him through their thoughts, words, and actions.
  - **Confront Shortcomings—**face up to the ways they are not growing closer to God.
  - **Look Toward the Day to Come—**ask God for the grace they need in the day to come.

  St. Ignatius of Loyola, who championed this form of prayer, recommends ending the daily Examen by praying the Lord's Prayer.

> **Whatever you are doing, that which makes you feel most alive, that is where God is.**
>
> —St. Ignatius of Loyola

Johnny had been misbehaving, and the catechist asked him to put his head down and pray for a few minutes. After a while, he lifted his head and told his catechist that he had thought it over and had then said a prayer. "Fine," said the pleased catechist. "If you ask God to help you not misbehave, He will help you." "Oh, I didn't ask Him to help me not misbehave," said Johnny. "I asked Him to help you put up with me."

- **Leading Reflective Prayer (Meditation)**—See the Reflect step in chapter 4.
- **Leading Liturgical Prayer**—Liturgical prayer is prayer that follows a more formal pattern with assigned parts for a leader, readers, and the assembly. Any liturgical prayer, or what we popularly refer to as a prayer service, resembles the Mass, and in doing so, deepens our desire to celebrate the Eucharist. Here are some things to keep in mind when planning and leading liturgical prayer:
    - **Check the Liturgical Calendar**—Through liturgical prayer, we pray with the whole Church, which means that we pay attention to the seasons and feasts of the Church year. This can be reflected in the theme of the prayer as well as in the words we pray, the songs we sing, and the way we prepare the prayer space.
    - **Create an Order of Service**—Since liturgical prayer is more formal and structured, it helps to create an order of service which in many ways is like a script or an outline for the prayer that indicates assigned parts, the flow of the prayer, songs and responses, and postures (sitting, standing, or kneeling). An order of service usually consists of some or all the following:
        - Song
        - Greeting and opening prayer
        - Liturgy of the Word (readings and responsorial Psalm)
        - Intercessions
        - Conclusion (Lord's Prayer, ritual action, closing prayer, song)

An Order of Service

Scan this QR code to download a PDF of a sample order of service.

- **Ask Yourself, "What Will the Group Be Doing?"**—In liturgical prayer, everyone has a role to play. This does not mean that every learner must have an individual role, but that the group as a whole entity is an active participant through singing, responding, listening, praying in silence, sharing traditional prayers, taking part in ritual action, and observing the advised postures.

- **Assign Roles ahead of Time**—Be sure that everyone knows his or her assigned part ahead of time and, if needed, has had an opportunity to prepare or rehearse. If you've assigned prayer parts such as "left" and "right" or "group 1" and "group 2," be sure to tell your learners ahead of time which side or group they belong to. If there is a ritual gesture that needs explaining (e.g., learners coming forward to bless themselves with holy water), give directions ahead of time so that the prayer can flow smoothly.

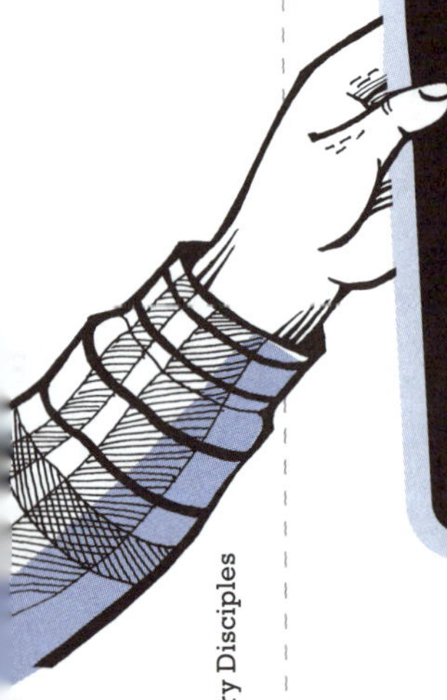

Building Familiarity with the Mass—By leading others in liturgical prayer and by incorporating prayers and actions from the Mass, we help to predispose learners to the transformation that the celebration of the Eucharist—the source and summit of the Christian life—offers. For more information about the Mass, see my book *Living the Mass: How One Hour a Week Can Change Your Life* (Loyola Press, 2005).

Leading Spontaneous Prayer—Spontaneous prayer actually follows a structure or pattern within which you speak to God without a prepared text. You can lead spontaneous prayer more easily if you keep these steps in mind, but without feeling the need to follow them rigidly:

- **Lead the Sign of the Cross**
- **Address God**—This may sound like stating the obvious, but it is important to begin a prayer by calling on God. We do so by using any one of a variety of divine titles that describe God (for example, Almighty God, Heavenly Father, Good and Gracious God).

Dear God

The *Catechism of the Catholic Church* teaches us that while we can direct prayer toward Jesus, prayer is primarily addressed to the Father (2680). For this reason, it is good to have a repertoire of divine titles or a personal favorite that you can rely on each time you lead spontaneous prayer.

- **Name God's Mighty Deeds**—Because our prayer is a response to the many wonderful things God has done for us, name one or more of God's great deeds—either in the past or in the present—(for example, "You created all things . . ." or "You sent us your only Son, Jesus . . ." or "You have brought us together today . . .").
- **Offer Thanks**—Immediately after naming something that God has done, it makes sense to offer thanks and praise—or, as we say at Mass, "It is right and just!" Here it makes sense to think of what everyone in the group is thankful for and to voice it. For example, "Thank you for bringing us together on this special occasion" or "Thank you for this opportunity to grow closer to you on this retreat."

It makes sense to offer thanks and praise—or, as we say at Mass, "It is right and just!"

- **Pray for the Needs of the Group or the Purpose of the Gathering**—Having addressed God and recalling and thanking him for his amazing deeds, present the group's needs to God, asking God for the grace the group needs at that moment.

Don't Get *Too* Specific!

When praying for the needs of the group, avoid asking for specific outcomes such as "We pray that our team captures the championship." Instead, consider praying for virtues and graces needed such as "We pray that you send your Holy Spirit upon our team to give them the grace they need to play hard, to play fair, and to show good sportsmanship."

- **Pray for the Needs of Others**—We never simply pray for ourselves, but we think of the needs of others, including those who are sick, those who were unable to be with the group, and for current needs that are on everyone's minds.
- **Conclude**—Make the prayer "through Jesus" or "in Jesus's name." This way, the prayer is Trinitarian: we address and praise the Father and recall his deeds, we ask the Holy Spirit to help us, and we make the prayer through Christ our Lord or in Jesus's name. Amen.

And that, my friends, is the anatomy of a spontaneous prayer!

"... and is there anything You could do to punch up Sunday School?"

Scripture

Rising very early before dawn, he left and went off to a deserted place, where he prayed. MARK 1:35

Prayer

Lord Jesus, you made prayer a regular part of your life and ministry. Time and again, the Scriptures tell us that you went off alone to pray. You knew that the Creator was your source of power. You knew that prayer was your link to the power of the Creator. Help me realize the power of prayer in my life and in the life of my learners. Teach us all to pray so that we may acknowledge your power and glory and be energized by your grace. Amen.

Chapter Ten

Sandpaper: Smoothing Out Discipline Problems

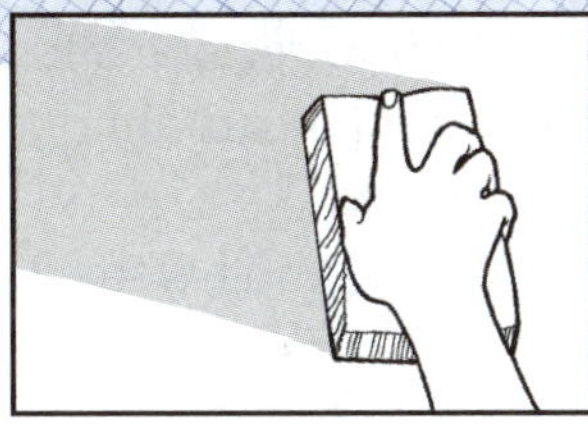

After filling cracks in a wall and allowing the spackling paste to dry, the surface will be rough and will need to be smoothed out with sandpaper. Left unchecked, discipline problems can be like a wall that has not been sanded. A good catechist learns how to smooth out discipline problems.

> **[The catechist] is called to look after the quality of the relationships and to foster the dynamics in the group being catechized.**
>
> —*Directory for Catechesis*, 150

Rough Edges in Catechesis: Group Dynamics and Discipline Problems

It is common to have a somewhat romantic notion of being a catechist. We may picture ourselves speaking eloquently as learners interact joyfully and enthusiastically with us and with one another. And then, of course, there is reality. In catechesis, we encounter any number of rough edges. One of the rough edges we face is that of complex group dynamics and, especially when working with young people, discipline problems. Maintaining discipline in the catechetical setting is essential because it allows the beauty of the learners and the power of God's word to show through, just as sanding down a surface brings out the true beauty of a piece of wood.

Rather than giving up when faced with discipline problems, you can learn how to use a number of tools to smooth them out. Discipline is a necessary part of faith formation. Think about it: each Lent, we practice the *disciplines* of prayer, fasting, and giving alms, knowing that to be a disciple of Jesus, one needs discipline. Remember, our God is "not the God

Jesus himself faced some rather difficult situations:

- Jesus was rejected in his hometown. (Matthew 13:57)
- The crowds challenged Jesus's authority. (Mark 11:28)
- Jesus was thrown out of the synagogue and dragged to a cliff. (Luke 4:29)
- A Samaritan town refused to receive Jesus. (Luke 9:52–53)
- The crowds grumbled when Jesus announced he would dine with Zacchaeus. (Luke 19:7)
- Many of Jesus's followers found his teaching too difficult and left him. (John 6:66)
- Crowds picked up stones to throw at Jesus. (John 8:59)
- The crowds challenged Jesus's healing of a man born blind. (John 9:16)
- More stones! (John 10:31)

of disorder but of peace" (1 Corinthians 14:33). When you maintain discipline in your learning environment, you are acting in the image of God—in whose name you teach.

- **Understand the Role of Discipline**—Good discipline is not itself an end. The goal of your session is to facilitate encounters with the risen Christ. A catechist can have good discipline but still create a poor faith formation experience. The role of good discipline is to remove any obstacles from truly encountering the Lord.
- **Make a Few Rules, and Explain and Enforce Them Fairly, Gently, and Consistently**—When you first begin meeting with your group, it is a good idea to formulate some rules with the help of the learners. Depending upon the age of your learners, you should be able to ask them what rules they will need to make the gatherings go well and to

Have you noticed the similarities between the words *discipline* and *disciple*? They both share the same root word, which means "to learn." In other words, as a catechist, you are responsible for keeping discipline so that disciples can learn how to follow Jesus.

create a good learning environment. Later, when enforcing the rules, you can remind them that these are their rules. Be sure learners know clearly what the rules are. Also, you should enforce them in a fair, gentle, and consistent manner, so the learners know that the rules are to be taken seriously.

- **Identify the Improper Behavior**—One doesn't need to sand down an entire wall before painting. Only the rough spots need to be sanded down. Similarly, be sure to clearly identify the discipline problems that you need to address. Be aware that some discipline problems may very well be related to mental health or emotional issues. Only after you have clearly identified the discipline problems that are most troublesome can you develop a plan for addressing them.

> **Discipline is not about control, punishment or rewards—it's about teaching.**
> —Jane Nelsen, *Positive Discipline*

- **Don't Panic or Erupt**—When discipline problems arise, strive to remain calm and in control. Communicating a sense of authority while remaining calm is not only effective but also necessary in developing a long-term strategy for combating discipline problems. Losing your cool may work for the moment, but it undermines your credibility in the long run. Avoid saying anything that disrespects the dignity of the individual.

- **Avoid Interrupting Yourself or the Lesson**—One of the reasons children and adolescents misbehave is because they know that their disruption will interrupt the flow of the lesson, frustrate you, and bring

Restorative Discipline

Research shows that traditional punitive responses to misbehavior are not effective in reducing disruptions. Meanwhile, research on alternative discipline approaches, including restorative justice and positive behavior intervention and support, show promise. Restorative discipline emphasizes responding to disruptive behavior by focusing on conflict resolution, acceptance of responsibility, and the rebuilding of relationships.

attention to them. A good catechist learns to deal with discipline problems without stopping the lesson. By using intense eye contact, placing a hand on the learner's desk or tabletop, or standing next to the disruptor while you continue to facilitate the lesson, you can minimize the behavior without interrupting the flow of your lesson.

- **Keep Learners Engaged**—When learners get bored, they try to create their own stimulation. When you see that a learner's attention is wavering, engage him or her in the lesson by asking a question or by giving the learner a task to perform. By keeping your learners engaged and on task right from the start, you eliminate a great deal of potential trouble.

By keeping your learners engaged and on task right from the start, you eliminate a great deal of potential trouble.

The Underlying Causes of Poor Behavior

Educational experts identify the following as some of the reasons why children misbehave:

> Unmet physical needs (lack of food, nutrition, sleep, medical issues)
> Lack of confidence and skills
> Boredom, not being sufficiently challenged or engaged
> Immaturity and ego needs (seeking attention, trying to impress peers, testing boundaries)
> Personality clash (hostility toward you, other learners, the Church, or parents)
> Emotional problem (family situation, guilt, inner conflict)
> The nature of religious formation in a secular world (young people, especially preadolescents and early adolescents, sometimes don't want their peers to think that they enjoy religion)

While some of these factors are out of your control, keeping learners engaged is one of the most effective ways of reducing misbehavior.

Scan the Room, Use Names, and Move Around—If you are completely stationary as a catechist, you invite the learners farthest away from you to engage in misbehavior. Stay on the move. Walk around and scan the room as you teach, making eye contact with learners. If you are answering one learner's question, move your eyes around the room so that it is clear you are still engaging everyone. Most important, learn and use your learners' names. One of the most effective ways of getting a learner's attention is to call his or her name aloud, pause, and direct the question or task to that person.

"I'm going to be a bit more authoritarian today than usual."

> **Be ever engaged, so that whenever the devil calls, he may find you occupied.**
> —St. Jerome

Check Your Seating Arrangement—How a space is arranged can have a significant impact on behavior. Your seating should be arranged in such a way that no learner feels separated or remote from the hub of activity. If a learner feels he or she can "hide" from you, he or she will take advantage of the situation. Make sure visual lines are open. Likewise, if a learner is misbehaving, it could be that he or she is sitting with others who are egging the learner on. Moving a learner's seat can effectively reduce unruly behavior.

- **Reinforce Good Behavior**—Don't just focus on the negative. Learn to focus attention on good behavior and reinforce it. When learners are behaving properly, you can reward them with affirmations. When a learner who is prone to misbehaving shows the proper behavior, be sure to reinforce it—without going overboard—with a positive affirmation.
- **Get to Know the Age Group You Work With**—Be sure to know the developmental characteristics of the age group you are working with. Some behaviors can be more easily understood and dealt with if you have a working knowledge of the physical, psychological, emotional, social, moral, and spiritual characteristics of the age group. Most catechist manuals and leader resources include an overview of these developmental characteristics.
- **Practice "Evangelizing" Discipline**—This means that instead of just correcting someone's behavior or telling them to be quiet, you take a moment to remind them why we are here—namely, to grow closer to Jesus Christ. You might also want to remind everyone what the moment properly calls for as far as our behavior. Some of you may have heard about teachable moments; this is a similar approach. But since we've created a climate of prayer, think of it as an evangelizing moment rather than a teaching moment.
- **Enlist Help When Necessary**—Finally, there may be times when misbehavior is so serious that you need to enlist the help of your catechetical leader (or, as a last resort, the pastor) to properly address the issue. Be sure to keep a paper trail of specific disruptive behaviors, when they happened, how often they happened, what the behavior entailed, how you handled it, and how the learner responded. This can go a long way in substantiating your side of the story and protecting yourself. Some situations can be addressed by drawing up and signing a contract or a period of probation that gives learners an opportunity to repair the damage their misbehavior has caused. Discipline is not about punishment; it is about restoring things to the way God intends.

Discipline is not about punishment; it is about restoring things to the way God intends.

A catechist confronted a misbehaving learner. "Didn't you promise to behave?" The learner said, "Yes." The catechist responded, "And didn't I tell you there would be consequences if you misbehaved?" The learner paused a second and then said, "Yes, but since I broke my promise, you don't have to keep yours."

Finally, with the knowledge of your catechetical leader, you may need to call a parent to enlist their help in talking to their child about a particular behavior. Again, keep good records and keep your catechetical leader informed of such conversations.

Avoid the Following

- Never send a child to the office alone and unsupervised, lest he or she wander off or even leave the building.
- Be careful not to use God as an enforcer. Some catechists use the good cop/bad cop routine, with God as the bad cop. This creates a theology of God that is not consistent with our heritage. Children do not benefit from an image of an angry God waiting to dish out punishment for unruly behavior.
- Avoid being overly tough; you run the risk of alienating your learners. They may be so intimidated that they will either not respond at all or will simply parrot back to you what they think you want to hear. Recall that faith formation is, for many learners, their most significant experience of the Church. If it is a negative experience, or one that they fear, they may carry this with them for years to come.

Effective Group Work

- Discipline problems often arise when learners are arranged in groups to complete a task. Here are some tips for working more effectively with small groups:
  - Provide clear instructions and directions *before* arranging them into groups.
  - Employ creative and fun techniques for creating groups, involving learners in the process.

- Give brief and concise time limits for completing the task.
- Provide a signal that will indicate when the groups are to quiet themselves and return their attention to the large group.
- Be sure that the group work cannot be completed by any one learner alone but truly requires each member of the group to assume responsibility for a task.
- Keep moving around the room to provide ongoing feedback (affirmations and challenges, as needed) as they continue their work.
- Make sure that the results of the group work are observable and concrete.

Facilitating Group Work

Scan this QR code to view a brief video of Joe sharing more information about effectively facilitating group work.

Do Adults Misbehave at Faith Formation Events?

Obviously, much of this chapter refers to the experience of working with children and teens who are, or should be, more prone to misbehave than adults. Does that mean that catechists who work with adults can expect perfect behavior? Not so fast! The truth is, adults are also capable of disruptive behavior. What's a catechist of adults to do? For starters, if you go back through this chapter, you will find that many of the strategies apply to all age groups. Likewise, many of the skills, tips, and strategies we discussed in chapter 7—Spotlights: Shifting the Focus onto Learners—will come in handy when dealing with disruptive behavior in an adult setting.

When working with adults, it is just as helpful to discuss ground rules at the outset as it is when working with children. Avoid being confrontational, and don't hesitate to treat situations with humor if the disruption is mild. Likewise, address the disruption discreetly and privately if possible. Know that most adult disruptive behavior will occur when they feel that their needs are not being met, so engagement is always key; don't allow adult learners to become passive, and be sure to articulate lofty expectations.

Finally, as the catechist, you are still in charge even if the other adults in the group are older than you! Be sure to assert your authority (again, without being authoritarian). You have a responsibility to the rest of the group to say something calmly but firmly (and at the proper time and place) about disruptive behavior, regardless of the person's age or status.

Scripture

Endure your trials as "discipline"; God treats you as sons. For what "son" is there whom his father does not discipline? . . . At the time, all discipline seems a cause not for joy but for pain, yet later it brings the peaceful fruit of righteousness to those who are trained by it. HEBREWS 12:7, 11

Prayer

Sometimes I get worried about having to face challenging situations in my teaching. Lord Jesus, you faced some tough audiences in your day. Yet you stayed focused on preaching the Good News of the kingdom of God. Grant me the patience, fairness, and perspective I need to maintain my focus, face up to these challenges, and handle them with calmness and authority. In all things, allow me to show love no matter how frustrated I may become. Help me acquire new skills to handle challenges so that your word may spring to life in my learners. Amen.

Chapter Eleven

Primer and Paint: Evangelization and Catechesis

Primer and paint work together to ensure maximum adhesion, increased durability, and greater protection for the painted surface. In faith formation, catechesis and evangelization work together to ensure that God's word "adheres" to hearts and minds to create a faith that is durable and protected from harm.

Catechesis must have a profound connection with evangelization.
—*Directory for Catechesis*, 322

Catechesis and Evangelization: A Profound Connection

In my early days of home improvement, I confess that I sometimes tried to get by without using primer before I painted. The results were that the paint did not adhere as well, the previous color bled through, and the paint job lacked durability. In a similar way, catechizing without evangelizing is like painting without using primer. Without evangelization, our catechesis will not penetrate and adhere to hearts and minds, and without catechesis, our evangelization efforts will not be protective or durable.

Catechizing without evangelizing is like painting without using primer.

Catechesis and evangelization work together like two dance partners who move together with such fluidity that they appear to move as one entity. In fact, once catechesis and evangelization begin working together, it is difficult to differentiate between the two movements. Thus, we can simply speak of "evangelizing catechesis," which is the focus of this chapter as we explore nine ways that our transmission of the gospel can and should lead to lives transformed by an ever-deepening relationship with Jesus Christ.

- **Explore Brokenness–**It is difficult to convince someone that they need a savior if they are convinced that they don't need saving or believe that they can save themselves. The first strategy of evangelizing catechesis is to invite learners to recognize that something is missing from their (our) lives or that the lives they (we) are living are broken and in need of repair. In other words, we draw attention to needs that learners know they have as well as needs that learners do *not* know they have. Our goal is not to point out people's flaws! Rather, we invite learners to recognize the hurt, pain, or emptiness that all people–including ourselves–are carrying around in one form or another.

  In short, proclaiming the Good News is most effective when we first draw attention to the bad news that is weighing us down. For example, if we are going to proclaim that Jesus is the Bread of Life and that he satisfies our hunger, it is most effective to explore the many ways in which we human beings hunger and how we, often at the urging of the world in which we live, attempt to satisfy that hunger in ways that may provide immediate gratification but are not life-giving and are perhaps even destructive.

- **Propose an Alternate Reality: Jesus Christ and the Kingdom of God–**By attending Twelve Step meetings, people struggling with addictions strive to learn a new way of being human, ridding themselves of unhealthy narratives and replacing them with a healthy, life-giving narrative. Evangelizing catechesis invites all of us to recognize that we are powerless over sin and learn a new way of being human as offered by Jesus Christ. The invitation to follow Jesus is the invitation to a change of scenery as we invite learners to relocate into the Kingdom of God–that place where God's vision for fullness of life reigns.

Let's Be Honest

It's no coincidence that the Mass begins with a Penitential Act in which we admit our brokenness and our need for salvation. Likewise, it is no coincidence that the first major section of the Mass, the Liturgy of the Word, proposes a new narrative for our lives. This flow can be found in the Twelve Step process for healing the brokenness caused by addiction. In our faith formation, we do well to reinforce this dynamic: we are broken, and we are in need of a new vision or narrative to guide our lives. By embracing our brokenness, we open ourselves up to grace.

The most effective way of proposing a new narrative is by sharing stories from Scripture, from the lives of the saints, and, most important, from our own lives that illustrate the transforming experience of encountering Christ. For countless people over many centuries, following Jesus has provided a way out of lives that were dead ends in favor of lives that offer hope and the promise of a better way.

> **I'm fairly convinced that the Kingdom of God is for the brokenhearted.**
> —Fred Rogers

"I can't preach, sing, or play a musical instrument, but, by George, I can teach up a storm!"

- **Show a Better Way**—The late Cardinal Francis George, OMI, once cleverly quipped that, "In the end, we are all from Missouri" (the "Show-Me State"). He went on to explain that it is human nature to insist on seeing proof of any claim. If we are going to effectively proclaim the Good News of Jesus, we need to in effect take the witness stand and offer testimony, which we do through our words and our actions, about what we have seen and heard regarding the amazing deeds of Jesus.

  When we proclaim the Good News of Jesus, we must remember that those to whom we are testifying may be thinking, *Show me, don't tell me!* It is up to us to tell the stories of Jesus's amazing deeds, beginning with the stories we have in Scripture and the lives of the saints as well as those we can tell from our own lives. We need to share how Jesus has transformed us, healed us (whether physically, emotionally, or spiritually), raised us to new life, and enabled us to live a better way.

- **Present the Paradox: The Better Way Requires "Dying"**—It is a peculiarity of Christianity that we invite people to new life by showing them a crucified man. The truth is, at the heart of the better way of Jesus is a great paradox: if you want to possess fullness of life, you must *lay down your life*. For us to effectively transform hearts and minds, we need to show learners how to lay down their lives for others, a process that begins with letting go of who you were and are in order to become a new person. One of the ways we do this is by learning to set our own needs aside in order to tend to the needs of others. Selfless love is the heart of the gospel message.

  The key to teaching others how to lay down their lives and become a new person is to apprentice them in works of mercy, or service to others. The *Directory for Catechesis* states boldly, "It becomes ever clearer that there is no proclamation of the faith if this is not a sign of God's mercy. The practice of mercy is already itself an authentic catechesis: it is catechesis in action" (51). It is through the practice of mercy that we die to our old selves and are born again in Christ.

- **Facilitate Encounters with the Risen Christ**—Cardinal Blase Cupich once said that the problem we face as a Church is not so much whether Catholics believe in the real presence of Jesus in the Eucharist, but rather whether we believe in the resurrection of Jesus.

> Theologian Stanley Hauerwas reminds us, "Our problem is very simple—we simply do not know how to live as people who believe that Jesus is the resurrected Lord."

Our entire belief system rests upon the belief that Jesus is risen from the dead. And yet, too often in our faith formation, we invite Jesus into our presence and then make him sit in the corner while we talk about him as if he weren't there.

What we need to do is invite the risen Christ into our presence. We enable encounters with him by creating a climate of prayer and by facilitating prayer experiences (as discussed in chapter 4) in which our learners speak with and listen to the risen Christ in a deep, profound, and intimate manner. In doing so, they learn how to search for and encounter Jesus in their daily lives.

Too often in our faith formation, we invite Jesus into our presence and then make him sit in the corner while we talk about him as if he weren't there.

- **Invite Learners to Have Experiences of This Better Way of Living**—People like to know what they are getting into. For that reason, it is especially helpful when someone we trust, admire, and respect invites us to test the waters. It is crucial for catechists to be on the lookout for the right time to invite learners to use their unique gifts to serve others and, by companioning with them, help them encounter Christ and experience a better way of being human.

Invitations like this can be transformative and even life changing. Think of times in your own life when a personal outreach led to a new friendship, a new hobby, your present job or career, your significant other, or a new home.

Invitations Can Change Lives

Scan this QR code to view a brief video of Joe sharing how invitations can change lives.

The Personal Touch

When it comes to invitations, surveys show that the personal touch can't be beaten. They make people feel seen, heard, and known, if not appreciated and valued. As a catechist, you can make a significant difference in the lives of those you teach by personally inviting them to take the next step, whatever that step may be, on their faith journey.

God's invitations often come through other people. As catechists, it is our responsibility to pass along God's call to our learners. We can do so by inviting learners to participate in a retreat experience; engage in service and works of mercy; collaborate on a project; participate in a liturgical ministry; join or lead a small group experience; serve as an aide; attend a workshop, seminar, rally, or conference to hear an inspirational speaker; or find a way to help people in need in their own communities.

> **If you have the opportunity to do amazing things in your life, I strongly encourage you to invite someone to join you.**
> —Simon Sinek

- **Appeal to the Mind *and* the Heart**—Evangelizing catechesis is much more than the delivery of doctrine. It is meant to appeal to the *whole* person, both mind and heart. One of the reasons that our faith formation too often falls flat is because it remains solely at the intellectual level. To entice people to consider following Jesus, we need to invite them to experience conversion, which, as it involves the letting go of old ways, is hastened by emotions. We need to invite learners to honestly get in touch with the sadness and despair of brokenness and emptiness even as we invite them to experience the joy, hope, and intimacy of discipleship with Jesus.

The new catechetical leader was relieved when she finished her first adult faith formation presentation. During the reception afterward, many people told her how much they enjoyed the presentation. One man, however, came up to her three different times. "That was really dull and boring," he said the first time. "I don't think you did much preparation for that presentation," he said the second time. And the third time, he said, "You didn't have anything worthwhile to share." The catechetical leader sought out one of her catechists and asked, "What's up with that guy? All he does is complain!" The catechist responded, "Oh, don't pay much attention to him. He's kind of quirky. He just goes around repeating what he hears everyone else saying."

⊕ **Marinate Learners in the Catholic Way of Life**—We learned a long time ago that *Just Say No!* is not an effective strategy for reducing drug use among young people. Similarly, evangelizing catechesis is about much more than simply inviting people to stop doing sinful things. It is about the work of helping learners to live differently. To follow Jesus requires us to reprioritize our lives. We do that by adopting a new philosophy and strategy for living in order to create a new lifestyle—or, in other words, to embark upon a better way of being human.

One of the most effective evangelizing strategies that a catechist can utilize is to immerse (I like to use the word *marinate*) learners in practices that characterize the way followers of Jesus think, speak, and act. Such practices include learning, memorizing, and praying Catholic prayers and devotions; performing sacramental actions such as blessing oneself; fasting; abstaining from meat; wearing sacramentals such as a scapular, medal, or cross; observing the liturgical seasons and feasts of the Church year; performing Corporal and Spiritual Works of Mercy; and reading Catholic literature. Over time, individuals will find themselves drawn to the practices that speak most powerfully to them.

The Right Kind of Heartburn

After Jesus listened to and then spoke with the two disciples on the road to Emmaus, they remarked, "Were not our hearts burning [within us] while he spoke to us on the way and opened the scriptures to us?" (Luke 24:32). They had developed the right kind of heartburn. The goal of evangelizing catechesis is to give people the kind of heartburn that we never want to go away and that no antacid will extinguish!

I firmly believe that our quest as catechists is to be preparing the next generation of our replacements.

Prepare Learners to Take Your Place—At the end of a conversation with a teen about his work as a catechist aide and his hope to become a catechist in a few years, I surprised him by saying, "Well, I'm glad I got to meet my replacement." When I saw his jaw drop, I added, "Hey, you never know!" I firmly believe that our quest as catechists is to be preparing the next generation of our replacements. The first step toward making this a reality is for us to stop thinking of those we teach as students and instead think of them as partners and collaborators whom we are mentoring and apprenticing so that they can one day take our place. We achieve this by affirming them, sharing our own stories, insights, and wisdom with them, and inviting them to participate in experiences that will make them feel part of a movement bigger than themselves.

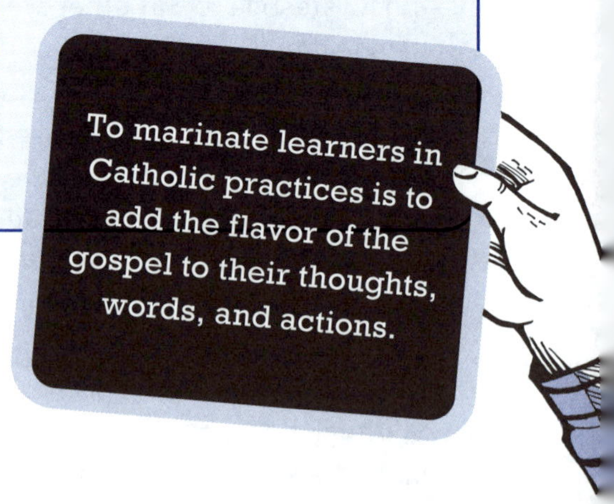

Scripture

And it happened that, while he was with them at table, he took bread, said the blessing, broke it, and gave it to them. With that their eyes were opened and they recognized him, but he vanished from their sight. Then they said to each other, "Were not our hearts burning [within us] while he spoke to us on the way and opened the scriptures to us?" LUKE 24:30–32

Prayer

Risen Christ, you listened to your two disciples on the road to Emmaus as they shared with you their grief and despair. You spoke to them about the meaning of Scripture and invited them to see a new reality. You broke bread with them and opened their eyes to your presence, upon which they exclaimed that you had set their hearts on fire. Help me spark that fire within the hearts of those I teach so that they, in turn, may go forth and set the world on fire! Amen.

Chapter Twelve

Furniture Polish: Polishing Your Technique

Typically, when I am done with a home improvement project, virtually everything in the vicinity is covered in a layer of dust. The next tool I turn to is some trusty furniture polish. As catechists, we need to continually polish our technique so that we are as effective as we can be.

> **Our falling short of perfection should be no excuse; on the contrary, mission is a constant stimulus not to remain mired in mediocrity but to continue growing.**
>
> —*Directory for Catechesis*, 138

Polishing Your Teaching Techniques

Many of us begin our work as catechists feeling stiff and inadequate. While some people seem very polished at public speaking, others of us may feel as though we are lacking in those skills. The following joke pokes fun at this reality:

As a visitor was touring a joke factory, he heard the supervisor call out over the loudspeaker, "Number seventy-two." This was followed by a roar of laughter from the workers. A minute later, he heard another announcement: "Number sixteen." Again, loud guffaws came from the workers. The visitor turned to the tour guide and asked, "What are they laughing at?" The tour guide explained, "The jokes are coded by number. When the supervisor calls out a number, everyone recognizes the joke, and that's why they laugh." The visitor asked, "Can I try it?" "Sure," replied the tour guide. The visitor went up to the microphone and called out, "Number sixty-eight." Nothing. No reaction. No laughter. "What happened?" he asked. The tour guide replied, "Well, I guess some people know how to tell a joke better than others."

It's true that not everyone has a polished technique when it comes either to speaking in public or telling jokes. The fact is, just as people can learn to give a speech or tell a joke, we catechists can polish our skills and techniques to become more effective at proclaiming the gospel and forming disciples of Jesus Christ. Let's look at some of the ways you can polish your technique as a catechist.

- **Move Around Your Learning Space**—Moving around the learning space while teaching helps keep learners on their toes and conveys positive energy and enthusiasm. It also expresses command of the learning space. Consider moving about in a way that makes you feel comfortable and also communicates good energy and enthusiastic acceptance.

> **We are evaluated and classified by these four contacts: what we do, how we look, what we say, and how we say it.**
> —Dale Carnegie

- **Make Eye Contact as You Scan the Room**—Your eyes should follow the same rule as your body—move around. As you move about the room, make sure that your eyes are scanning the group and you are making eye contact so all learners know that you are aware of them and interested in engaging them in the session. This is also an effective way of preventing misbehavior. By (almost) having eyes in the back of your head, you keep learners on task.
- **Vary Your Voice**—Few things are more boring to learners than a monotonous voice. Be sure to put some energy into your delivery. Use your voice as a tool to make a point or to add authority and enthusiasm to your lesson. Modulate your voice to make sure that it is not monotonous because if your own voice does not communicate interest in your topic, you have little chance of getting the learners interested. Use sufficient volume while avoiding extremes of too quiet or too loud.
- **Be Aware of Facial Expressions and Body Language**—People, especially children, are very attuned to facial expressions and body language. If we are truly preaching and teaching the Good News, then our faces and body language must reflect it. If our facial expressions and body language (including the way we dress) express the fact that we are tired, bored, irritated, or disinterested, then we are defeating ourselves. Use facial expressions and body language as a way of communicating that you truly have good news to share with your learners.

If we are truly preaching and teaching the Good News, then our faces and body language must reflect it.

The Eyes Have It

Research shows that when people make direct eye contact for at least 30 percent of a conversation, they recall more of what the other person said. If you want your learners to retain more of what you are saying, be sure to make direct eye contact. Experts recommend holding eye contact for no more than four to five seconds at a time to avoid making the other person uncomfortable.

One of the best ways to assess your movement, pace, voice, and facial expression is to record a video of yourself while you are teaching. Afterward, perhaps with the help of a colleague, assess your style.

- **Vary Your Pace**—Any runner will tell you that it is important to have a healthy pace for a distance run. Go too fast, and you'll run out of steam. Go too slow, and you fall behind. The same holds true of leading faith formation sessions. An effective catechist pays attention to pace. Be sure to keep an eye on the time to make sure you're not spending too much time on one segment at the expense of others. Similarly, if you are moving too quickly, slow down and include more detailed information to fill in the time.
- **Keep a Sense of Humor**—You don't have to become a comedian or an entertainer to be a good catechist; however, most people enjoy having fun, too. Humor is a way of celebrating, and, as Christians, we celebrate the Good News of Jesus. A few light moments in your sessions can make learners feel at ease. Appreciate the humor that your learners can offer and don't feel shy about adding your own. Strive to be professionally delightful. One can keep order and focus as a catechist and still maintain a sense of humor.
- **Be Aware**—When hockey legend Wayne Gretzky was asked for the key to his success, he explained that he had a knack for knowing where the puck was going and made sure he was there before anyone else. In other words, he had an awareness of what was going on and was able to anticipate the next move. An awareness of how your session is unfolding and how your learners are reacting is an important skill that will assist you in communicating the right thing at the right time.

An awareness of how your session is unfolding and how your learners are reacting is an important skill that will assist you in communicating the right thing at the right time.

- **Strive to Be Not Only Effective, but Also Affective—**In order to be an effective catechist, it helps to be an affective catechist. This is not to say that, as a catechist, you must wear your heart on your sleeve or force emotion out of learners in a manipulative manner (something that should never be done). Rather, it means not being afraid to express and invite the honest expression of the emotions that are integral to a life of discipleship. Expressing authentic emotion can humanize you and make you seem more accessible to your learners.

"Wait! Wait! He doesn't stay dead!"

Polish Your Storytelling Techniques

One of the most effective techniques for a catechist to employ is that of storytelling. Stories are effective because they are interesting and accessible. They reveal who God is and who we are in relation to God. Stories convey meaning, stress the initiative of God, introduce God-language, create images, lead to insights and action, and ultimately, lead us to faith. Storytelling is contagious; it leads to further storytelling. Take the following into consideration when storytelling:

- Prepare in advance and know the story well.
- Create a world that listeners can enter into by using their imaginations.
- Use nonverbal communication (eye contact, facial expressions) and involve the audience.
- Use your voice as a tool, consider your posture, and move about the space.

Succeeding as an Introvert

Scan this QR code to view a brief video of Joe sharing thoughts about how introverts can succeed in public speaking.

Giving Clues

Is nonverbal communication really all that important? Well, research shows that we nonverbally send messages to others by our appearance, posture, and facial expressions and that these expressions provide further cues to meaning. In fact, some researchers conclude that nonverbal communication accounts for up to two-thirds of all meaning. Take advantage of the many ways you can reinforce your message through nonverbal communication.

- Storytelling is not just a matter of reading a story; you need to tell a story with your voice. That means paying attention to volume (rising and falling to create drama) as well as pace, silence, pauses, and tone.

A New Narrative

As catechists, we weave a narrative that our learners can enter—a narrative of rescue, restoration, and reassurance. This narrative continuously describes God acting in the lives of his people down through the ages. This is why we tell stories not only from Scripture but also from the lives of the saints and from our own lives. This means that we need to tell stories of what Jesus has done for us when we have experienced powerlessness, pain, emptiness, anxiety, despair, and so on, as well as how we have encountered him in moments of great joy—any experience that led to a significant transition in our lives.

If you and I are going to be evangelizing catechists, we need to pause and ask ourselves, "What great things has Jesus done for me?" and then we need to tell those stories. Spend some time in prayer, asking Jesus to help you see the ways he has touched your life, transformed you, and healed you. Then ask him to help you tell your story, and invite others to get in touch with their own stories.

Getting in Touch with Your Story

To be better storytellers, each of us needs to become more aware of our own story. Here are some tips for getting in touch with your own story:

- **Identify Significant People in Your Life.** God typically speaks to us through other people. Who are the significant people in your life who have shaped and influenced you? The people to whom you owe a great deal? No doubt once you think of these significant people, you will recall stories related to their impact on your life.
- **Identify Moments of Joy (Big or Small).** Encountering God typically is a joyful experience. It makes sense, then, that we can recognize encounters with God by reflecting on moments of joy, whether big or small. In doing so, we can recognize and tell stories about God's movement in our lives.
- **Identify Peak Moments of Grace.** Most of us can think of a handful of extraordinary moments when we felt that God's presence was almost palpable. Perhaps it was a brush with death, a moment of incredible luck or fortune, a dramatic recovery from an unfortunate situation, or an extraordinary experience of beauty. Moments like these make us aware of a power greater than our own and make for inspiring stories.

The Three Rs: Rescue, Restoration, Reassurance

The Good News that we proclaim is a narrative that provides a new context for our lives. I mentioned earlier that this narrative can be summarized by what I call the three Rs:

- Rescue
- Restoration
- Reassurance

I've no doubt that the reason so many people love the song "Amazing Grace" is that it tells the story of how God's amazing grace rescues, restores, and reassures us.

But I Don't Have a Story!

Oh, yes, you do! Too often, we catechists think that we don't have a story to tell, mainly because our stories do not include voices from heaven, thunder and lightning, or apparitions. The truth is, all you need to do is share a story about how some aspect of your life is different because of Jesus. A good place to begin is to tell the story of how and why you became a catechist! You're doing something now that you didn't do before . . . and it's because of Jesus!

- **Identify milestones in your life.** Each of us can identify significant moments when we reach a milestone: a graduation, a new job, a promotion, a birthday or anniversary, a wedding day, and so on. These events cause us to pause and express gratitude, and when we express gratitude, we find ourselves contemplating the Giver of all good gifts.

The New Evangelization, if it is to be effective, must be couched in the context of our own personal stories. People do not want to be lectured about principles of dogma. However, they very well may want to hear a story about an everyday life experience in which God's nearness is revealed.

Polish Your Gifts

Think back to the joke factory story at the beginning of this chapter—some have natural technique, and some don't. God has given you both gifts and limitations. Become aware of them. Accentuate the positive. Play to your strengths. Highlight and improve upon the best that you have. Accept your limitations. As hard as we may try, some of us will just never be the next Archbishop Sheen. However, you can certainly reach your own unique potential!

> **If the truth were self-evident, eloquence would be unnecessary.**
> —Cicero

Scripture

Then they came to Capernaum, and on the sabbath he entered the synagogue and taught. The people were astonished at his teaching, for he taught them as one having authority and not as the scribes. MARK 1:21–22

Prayer

You must have had a very polished approach, Lord, because when you spoke, the crowds were astonished. They said that you "spoke with authority." Your Good News is still astonishing, and your word carries authority. Help me as an instrument of your grace to polish my technique and use the gifts you've given me to bring out the power of your word. Never let me stand in the way of your word or dull its power through my own complacency. Rather, polish my technique that I may allow the energy and enthusiasm of your Good News to leave my learners astonished by your teachings. Amen.

Chapter Thirteen

Instruction Manuals: Using Catechetical Resources

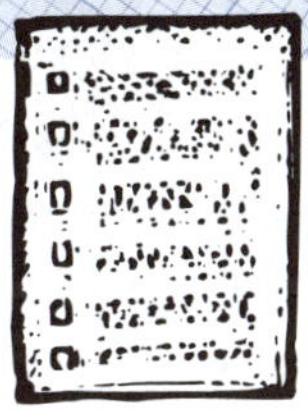

I have learned (the hard way) to follow instruction manuals when assembling, installing, or repairing anything (especially if it involves electricity or plumbing!). Catechists rely on quality resources, including catechist manuals and leader guides, to ensure that faith formation is faithful, comprehensive, age-appropriate, and utilizes effective pedagogy and methodology.

Although pre-eminent, it [the local catechism] is not supreme: other more immediate tools and resources are in fact necessary.
—*Directory for Catechesis*, 402

Using Catechetical Resources

When attempting certain home improvement projects, I sometimes find myself in over my head. If I want to get the job done properly, I make sure to consult instruction manuals and online tutorials. In a similar way, when it comes to faith formation, we catechists may find ourselves lacking certain knowledge of the Catholic faith or, at least, lacking the right words to effectively communicate the faith to our learners.

Over the years, I have encountered no small number of catechists who boldly proclaim that they don't need a catechetical textbook or other resource to do faith formation. Some go so far as to suggest that we do away with catechetical texts and just let catechists teach from the heart. While I admire the sentiment and have argued throughout this book that the heart of the catechist is indeed critical to faith formation, I will now also argue strongly that most catechists absolutely need some kind of quality catechetical resource to assist them in proclaiming the gospel fully and faithfully.

We are responsible for transmitting God's revelation fully and faithfully.

While catechesis is more about transformation than it is about information, it *does* involve specific, critical information. Through specific words and actions recorded in Scripture and expounded upon in our Tradition, our God has revealed what we need to know to encounter him and be transformed by his grace. We are responsible for transmitting God's revelation fully and faithfully.

To ensure that this transmission is indeed full and faithful, the Subcommittee on the Catechism of the U.S. Conference of Catholic Bishops conducts a rigorous conformity review process of printed catechetical resources to be used in faith formation programs. So unless you can guarantee that all the words that come out of your mouth and all the images you share are:

- age-appropriate and developmentally sound,
- faithful (in conformity) to the hundreds of goals outlined in the *Handbook on the Catechetical Accompaniment Process* issued by the U.S. bishops' Institute on the Catechism,
- properly Christocentric and Trinitarian,
- sufficiently emphasize God's initiative,
- properly emphasize the divinity of Christ,
- provide sufficient recognition of the transformative effects of grace,
- sufficiently treat original sin and sin in general,
- provide a robust presentation of the Christian moral life as well as an adequate presentation of eschatology,
- address all five tasks of catechesis, and
- present an authentic and distinctive Christian anthropology,

I would encourage you to hang on to (and use) the approved catechetical resource that your faith community/catechetical leader has provided you with.

Conformity with the *Catechism*

If you are wondering how to verify that a catechetical resource has been found by the U.S. bishops to be in conformity with the *Catechism of the Catholic Church*, consult the "Conformity Review List" at www.usccb.org.

In my experience, those who decide to catechize without using any kind of catechetical resource usually end up either doing most of the talking during their session or allowing the learners to do all the talking without adding any input, both of which are just as undesirable as constantly reading from a textbook. The most important resource, first and foremost, is *you*, the catechist. However, the effective catechist arrives prepared with the help of a variety of quality resources to ensure a full and faithful presentation of the faith.

Printed Textbooks Are Not Going Away

Whereas digital music made vinyl records and CDs dramatically decline, printed textbooks continue to remain popular among students of all ages. Experts predict that, when it comes to books, print will remain the dominant format for many years to come. Students list the following reasons for preferring print over eTextbooks:

- Print textbooks are easier to read.
- Students have trouble concentrating on eTextbooks.
- Students prefer to physically highlight passages.
- Internet access is not required.
- Print textbooks are easier to navigate and bookmark.

Research also shows that reading on a screen tends to be "shallower," while reading a text on paper results in greater comprehension and retention. It would seem that, when it comes to reading, going completely digital is akin to throwing the baby out with the bathwater.

Getting to Know Your Resources

It will serve you well to get to know your catechetical resources—no matter what those may be—as well as all their ancillary resources. Whether you are using a textbook, a video series, or an online resource, be sure to become familiar with the program's "scope and sequence"—a chart that outlines the resource's contents, themes, and the sequence in which they are presented.

Whatever your main method of delivering content may be, remember that these resources cannot replace you! The *Directory for Catechesis* (190) reminds us that the *Catechism* and all other catechetical resources require a mediator. As the catechist, you are the mediator: the most important resource in the faith formation setting since you are the spiritual mentor for a group of apprentices. You are the one who can and must relate stories of your own experiences about how you have sought to live as a disciple of Christ. Books, videos, online resources, worksheets, and more are available to provide concrete and accurate information about our faith heritage, but only you can share stories and insights about how that faith has transformed you in your daily life and how it can do the same for those you teach.

You are the one who can and must relate stories of your own experiences about how you have sought to live as a disciple of Christ.

Truth is, chances are slim you will be able to cover everything in the resource you've been provided, which means that you, under the guidance of the Holy Spirit and with the help of your catechetical leader and fellow catechists, will need to make decisions about which content to cover and in what sequence.

Let's look at some tips for using catechetical resources more effectively.

- **Familiarize Yourself with Your Catechetical Resource**—Take the time to go through the entire content of your catechetical resource well before you begin teaching to become familiar with the overall theme, as well as unit and chapter themes. Most catechist manuals and leader guides include a scope and sequence that identifies what doctrine is being presented in each grade throughout the program. It helps to know what was taught previously (even though that's no guarantee that learners received or retained that content) and what is going to be taught next year and beyond.

- **Know the Level of Aptitude of Your Learners**—Be sure your catechetical resource is appropriate for the age level and aptitude of your learners. Your catechetical leader or principal will no doubt play a significant role in this, but you are the one in the trenches. As a catechist, be sure that your resource is a tool that will assist, not frustrate, your learners. Furthermore, most catechist manuals and leader guides include materials that help you understand the developmental aspects (physical, social, psychological, moral, and spiritual) of the age group you are working with. Read up on this background information so that you are more in tune with your learners.

As a catechist, be sure that your resource is a tool that will assist, not frustrate, your learners.

- **Preview the Material You Plan to Cover**—Some catechetical resources are so good that they can lull us into a false sense of complacency. Beware of this pitfall. Carefully preview the material you plan to cover in each session to ensure that it is an effective lesson and that it fits within the time frame you have. Consider how you personally will add to and expound on what it delivers. Strive to memorize the learning outcomes for each session you are about

By failing to prepare, you're preparing to fail.
—Benjamin Franklin

to teach so that they are on the tip of your tongue. Keep abreast of current events for stories and images that relate to the theme of your session.

- **Give Your Learners an Overview of What They Are about to Read or View**—Catechists commonly make the mistake of beginning a lesson with instructions such as "Open your book to page thirty-five. Can I have a volunteer to read?" or "Okay, let's watch this video." The first problem is that the learners have no notion of what the goal for the lesson is other than to read the text or watch a video. The second problem is that the learners have no concept of what they are supposed to pay attention to, zero in on, or look for in the text or video.

Vary Your Approach—Material in a text or video can be accessed in a variety of ways. Here's one example:

> **Paired Interviews**—Arrange learners in pairs and assign half of the text to one learner and the other half of the text to the other (or, if a video, assign responsibility for the first half of the video to one learner and responsibility for the last half to the other).
>
> - Provide an interview sheet with questions such as: What is the main idea of your section? What is a key word from your section? What does the key word mean? What is the most inspiring sentence/comment/idea from your section? What is one idea from your section that all Catholics should know or do?
> - Before learners read their assigned sections or view the video, have them look over the interview questions so that they know what to look for as they read or view.
> - Have them read their assigned sections silently or view the video, taking note of the information needed for the interviews.
> - Then, invite the learners to take turns interviewing one another about what they read or viewed, using the interview sheet.
> - Invite the pairs to share with the large group, each child reporting on what his or her partner read as you highlight and emphasize essential information.

When reading or working on a section of a text or when showing a video or reviewing online information, an introduction and a brief overview of what learners are about to read, view, or encounter is advisable. This helps the learners become predisposed to pay attention.

Vary Your Approach

Scan this QR code to view a brief video of Joe offering ideas for how to vary your approach to accessing content from a textbook or video.

Identify Vocabulary Words and Key Phrases– If your catechist manual or leader guide has not already done so, identify words that should become part of your learners' vocabulary, as well as key phrases or ideas that should be highlighted. Previewing your catechetical resources ahead of time allows you to identify these words and phrases and place them on the board, in a slide, or on a newsprint pad for quick reference. Building a faith vocabulary (religious literacy) is an important aspect of equipping learners to talk about their faith to others.

Nothing is pleasant that is not spiced with variety.
—Francis Bacon

A catechist who was a bit rough around the edges directed his learners to read a few pages of the textbook about the Ten Commandments and then gave a quiz, which he quickly graded and returned. He reviewed the quiz questions with the group and then asked for questions. One young learner said, "I don't think I deserved a zero on this quiz." The catechist responded, "I agree, but that's the lowest mark I could give."

Religious Literacy

According to Pew Research, when it comes to religious literacy in America, Jews, atheists, agnostics, and evangelical Protestants tend to outperform members of other Protestant traditions, Catholics, and Mormons. We Catholics must get better at being able to talk knowledgably about religion.

- **If Reading from a Text, Be Aware of the Pace of Your Session—** Reading from a text can slow down the pace of your session. Break up the reading of text by interspersing activities and discussions that will ensure that your learners remain engaged.
- **Carefully Look Over the Catechist Notes in Your Manual or Leader Guide—**Most catechist manuals and leader guides provide liner notes or a section in the margin of each page containing background on the text and suggestions for discussing and exploring the content. These catechist notes can provide you with some excellent ideas for making the text come alive and connecting it with your learners' lives. Feel free to add your own notes to the ones provided.
- **Develop Additional Questions and Activities—**Use your catechist manual or leader guide as a springboard for adding your own discussion questions and learning activities. Draw attention to any graphics (photographs, pictures, and artwork) that accompany the text you are exploring and generate additional questions and discussion related to them. Look over any worksheets, activity sheets, or online activities that are provided as supplements to your catechetical resource and determine when and how they can be most effectively used.

"How come I've never heard any of this on 'Sesame Street'?"

You Don't Have to Reinvent the Wheel

Catechists who decide to catechize without the assistance of an approved catechetical resource often burn out quickly due to the fact that they find themselves continually reinventing the wheel, creating resources from scratch that are readily available from various Catholic sources. Catechetical resources are there to assist, not confine, you. And, while resources come with recommendations for how to use them, you should feel free to creatively adapt those resources to your own style and approach.

Scripture

He came to Nazareth, where he had grown up, and went according to his custom into the synagogue on the sabbath day. He stood up to read and was handed a scroll of the prophet Isaiah. He unrolled the scroll and found the passage where it was written: "The Spirit of the Lord is upon me . . ." LUKE 4:16–18

Prayer

Lord, when you entered the synagogue in Galilee, you were handed the text, and you read from the prophet Isaiah. But you didn't stop there. You added a new insight or twist to the centuries-old text, and stirred up a great deal of controversy. Help me go beyond the texts that are handed to me and stir up something of interest to my learners so that they, too, may be challenged. Help me use the texts assigned to me as a catalyst or stepping stone to the fullness of your word—a word that does not simply fill space on a page but has the capacity to change lives forever. Amen.

Chapter Fourteen

How-To Videos: Turning to the Bible for Guidance

When doing home repairs or improvements, one of the most valuable tools at our fingertips is the ability to watch online how-to videos that show everyday folks grappling with the same project we wish to undertake. In faith formation, we turn to Scripture to see how, throughout salvation history, everyday people have grappled with the call to holiness.

> **Catechesis draws its message from the Word of God, which is its main source. Therefore, it is essential that the revealed word radically enrich our catechesis and all our efforts to pass on the faith.**
>
> —*Directory for Catechesis*, 91

Thank Goodness for How-To Videos

Where would we be without online how-to videos? I have used such videos to learn how to install ceiling fans, put together and operate a snow blower, and repair a damaged lawn. What I like most about these videos is that they are made by everyday people who have grappled with the project that I am undertaking. Thus, I benefit from their experience. In a similar way, Scripture is a collection of stories of how ordinary (as well as extraordinary) people have grappled with the challenge of living a life of holiness. We turn to their stories to see how to avoid their failures and how to emulate their successes.

Scripture is a collection of stories of how ordinary (as well as extraordinary) people have grappled with the challenge of living a life of holiness.

In faith formation, we are helping learners grapple with the call to live as disciples of Jesus: someone who discerns and follows God's will. Since we learn by example, it makes sense that we provide examples of people throughout salvation history who have sought to follow God's will. This is where the Bible comes in. The Bible provides us with numerous examples of what it looks like when human beings hear God's call, respond (either affirmatively, hesitantly, or negatively), and struggle to follow the will of God in their lives. Let's take a look at how you as a catechist can more effectively incorporate Scripture into your faith formation experiences.

- **Familiarize Yourself with the Bible**—If you wish to introduce learners to the Bible, make sure that you yourself are deepening your familiarity with Sacred Scripture. While it's nice to have a large Bible enthroned in your home for decorative purposes, it is also helpful to have a personal copy such as a softcover New American Bible (the translation used in the Lectionary) that you will actually pick up and read regularly, while also feeling free to highlight and write notes in the margins. Ask your catechetical leader, principal, or pastor to assist you in acquiring one if you don't already possess a personal Bible.

Overcoming Bibliophobia

Scan this QR code to view a brief video in which Joe explains how Catholics need to overcome "bibliophobia"—fear of the Bible!

- **Read and Pray the Bible**—It's not necessarily advisable to read the Bible as you would other books (i.e., beginning on page one and trying to get all the way through to the last page). Since the Bible is a collection of books, you can begin with any book that you are interested in. I recommend starting with the Book of Exodus in the Old Testament since it is the defining moment in the relationship between God and his Chosen People. In the New Testament, a good place to start is the Acts of the Apostles, which gives you a hint of the excitement and spirit of the early Church. You can then go back and read one of the four Gospels (Mark is easiest since it is the shortest).

A father was reading Bible stories to his young son. He read, "The man named Lot was warned to take his wife and flee out of the city, but his wife looked back and was turned to salt." His son asked, "What happened to the flea?"

- **Enthrone the Bible in Your Learning Space—**Make sure that the Bible is placed prayerfully in a prominent place in your learning space. To enthrone the Bible means to carry it reverently in procession to the prayer table before placing it on a Bible stand (surrounded by a cross and a candle or other sacred objects), so that it is in a place of honor and prominence for your faith formation session.
- **Arrange for Accessibility to Bibles for Your Learners—**Work with your catechetical leader or parish staff to make sure that Catholic Bibles are available for use in your learning space. Ideally, all your learners should have access to a Catholic Bible (whether in print or in digital format) each time you gather.
- **Incorporate Scripture into Your Faith Formation Sessions Regularly—**This is nonnegotiable. The *Directory for Catechesis* (90) refers to Scripture as having a place of "pre-eminence" in faith formation. God's word is central to the proclamation of the kingdom. Don't allow the Bible to simply be a "decoration," and don't limit the Bible to perfunctory prayer segments. Ground your entire lesson in Scripture. And when your textbook or other catechetical resource refers to a Scripture passage, invite your learners to locate the passage in the Bible and have one of the learners read the passage aloud from the enthroned Bible in your prayer space.

Each year, the third Sunday of January is set aside as Sunday of the Word of God, a day that invites Catholics to deepen their appreciation of God's word in Scripture and to celebrate, study, and proclaim the word of God to all. Catechists can use this occasion to invite learners to grow closer to God through Sacred Scripture.

Steps for Reading and Praying the Bible—In essence, we don't just read the Bible; we pray the Bible. Here are tips for reading and praying the Bible:

> Set a prayerful, quiet mood.
> Pray to the Holy Spirit to open your mind and heart to the word of God.
> Select and read a passage. Look over any footnotes and commentary that will assist your understanding of the passage.
> Go back and read the passage again, this time more slowly and prayerfully. If the passage describes a story or event, use your imagination to place yourself within the scene as a learner. Pause at phrases, words, or images that speak to you and allow them to resonate within your heart. Whereas your first read-through is for the head, this one is for the heart.
> Allow for some quiet time to let the word of God continue to echo in your heart, mind, and soul.
> Pray in your own words. Thank God for his word and ask for the grace you need to apply it to your life.

Ignorance of Scripture is ignorance of Christ.
—St. Jerome

Bring Bible Stories to Life—Select stories and passages that can be either proclaimed creatively, dramatized, role-played, drawn, or viewed on video. It is important that learners, especially children, see or hear these stories come to life so that they can begin making connections to their own life experiences and circumstances.

Use the Lectionary as a Guide—In addition to the Bible passages recommended by your catechetical resource, you can consider incorporating the Scripture readings

"Okay, four-year-olds! Let's polish off the book of Leviticus!"

> **The Holy Bible is like a mirror before our mind's eye. In it we see our inner face. From the Scriptures we can learn our spiritual deformities and beauties. And there too we discover the progress we are making and how far we are from perfection.**
>
> —Pope St. Gregory the Great

for the upcoming Sunday, following the cycle of readings in the Lectionary. You can use a resource such as "The Sunday Connection" at www.loyolapress.com to prepare your learners for the readings that will be proclaimed at Mass the following Sunday. This will help your learners become more familiar not only with the Bible but also with the church's liturgical cycle.

- **Teach Bible Skills**—Help your learners become more proficient in using the Bible. Teach them how to use biblical citation (for example, 1 Peter 2:3-4 represents the First Letter of Peter, chapter 2, verses 3 through 4). Demonstrate how to use the table of contents in the Bible to locate books. Have your learners participate in Bible searches by locating passages in the Bible and summarizing what they find. Use the Bible Bookmarks provided in my book *The Bible Blueprint* to help your learners better navigate the Bible and build familiarity with Bible stories and characters.

Interpreting Scripture

One of the most critical tasks facing catechists today is the need to help learners understand how to read and interpret Scripture within the Catholic Tradition. Some Christians believe that because the Bible is the inspired word of God and is inerrant, every word, phrase, and passage of the Bible must be interpreted literally. This approach, called fundamentalism, does not distinguish between truth and fact. A fundamentalist would say that if the Bible tells us that a large fish swallowed Jonah, then it literally happened. This literal approach to interpreting the entire Bible is fraught with problems that limit the reader's ability to apply the truths to contemporary experience.

According to *Life* magazine, the single most important event in the second Christian millennium was when Gutenberg printed the Bible. Today, of course, the Bible is also available in digital formats for easy access. Either way, be sure to give Scripture a preeminent place in your faith formation experiences.

God's Library

The Bible is not really a book but a collection of books that I like to call God's Library. The Bible is organized into the following sections:

The Old Testament—God's relationship with Israel before the birth of Jesus

- **Pentateuch** (Genesis through Deuteronomy)—the beginnings of God's relationship with Israel (with the Exodus story as the defining moment)
- **History** (Joshua through 2 Maccabees)—the centuries-long story of the forming and eventual downfall of the kingdoms of Israel and Judah
- **Wisdom** (Job through Sirach)—a collection of the wisdom and prayers of the people of Israel over many centuries
- **Prophets** (Isaiah through Malachi)—the teachings of the Prophets who challenged and encouraged the people of Israel

The New Testament—God's relationship with his people after the birth of Jesus

- **Gospels** (Matthew through John)—the four portraits of the life, teachings, actions, suffering, death, Resurrection, and Ascension of Jesus Christ
- **Acts of the Apostles** (Acts of the Apostles)—a sequel to the Gospel of Luke that provides an account of the experience of the early Church
- **Letters** (Romans through Jude)—the communications of the early Church (with a majority attributed to St. Paul) intended to build up various faith communities
- **Revelation** (Revelation)—a vision attributed to St. John of the ultimate battle between good and evil and the assurance that good will prevail

Catholics also believe in the Bible's inerrancy, but in relation to religious truth, not necessarily historical and scientific information. In other words, for example, the story of Jonah and the large fish teaches us divine truths, without error, about our relationship with God. It does so, however, using an allegorical (nonliteral) approach that does not pretend to be historically or scientifically accurate as we understand those fields of study today. Other examples that fit under this category of allegory/nonliteral include the creation accounts and the story of Noah's Ark (although most likely based on an historical event), both of which are considered by scholars as "pre-history."

Catholics do not use a *fundamentalist* approach to the Bible but rather a *contextualist* approach. A contextualist approach looks at the whole passage in context and determines what meaning or truth is being conveyed beyond the facts of the story. In other words, Catholics believe that everything in the Bible is *true*, although not everything in the Bible can be considered *fact*. Thus, a contextualist would not be as concerned with the issue of whether Jonah was factually swallowed by a large fish as with the essential truth being conveyed in the story that running away from God's will is futile and can be likened to being swallowed up in the darkness.

Catholics believe that everything in the Bible is *true*, although not everything is the Bible can be considered *fact*.

Who's Gonna Tell Him?

A few years back, after teaching a group of sixth graders about the first story of creation in the Book of Genesis, I paused and asked, "So, is this what you've been taught in science class?" The kids froze for a moment and looked at one another, as if they were all thinking, *Who's gonna tell him that this is not how it happened?* Eventually, one student responded, "No, we learned about the Big Bang theory and the theory of evolution," as all the other learners nodded their heads. I didn't let up but instead asked, "So, who's telling you the truth: your science teacher or me?" Again, there was a nervous silence as they looked at one another wondering who would be brave enough to tell me that the universe was not created in six days.

In his book *Religion and Science*, the late Ian Barbour, a scholar of science and religion, proposed four ways that science and faith can relate:

- **Conflict:** Science and biblical literalism are pitted against each another.
- **Independence:** Science and faith serve completely different purposes and do not overlap.
- **Dialogue:** Science and faith enter into dialogue to identify points of contact and areas where some overlap and correlation occurs.
- **Integration:** Science and faith interact and speculate about meaning with some integration possible.

It is crucial for catechists to move away from the first two models (conflict and independence). Instead, we should engage learners in the practice of exploring dialogue and integration between science and faith. As Pope Francis put it, "There cannot and must not be any opposition between faith and science" (video message to "Science for Peace" event, July 2-3, 2021).

Finally, I came clean and told them I was just messing with them and that I wanted them to know that *both* of us were teaching them the truth. I said, "Your science teacher is teaching you scientific truth. I am teaching you religious truth. Your science teacher is helping you explore the *how* of our world, while I am helping you explore the *why* of our existence." I stated firmly that the idea of science versus faith is a false choice.

The idea of science versus faith is a false choice.

I consider this discussion about the relationship between science and faith to be one of the most important discussions a catechist can have with twenty-first century learners. Pew Research Center tells us that learners as young as the age of ten are dismissing faith in favor of science because they perceive "church types" as viewing science and faith in conflict, whereas they, the learners, are concluding that science wins that battle because it simply makes more sense to them than what they perceive as fairy tales. They are reaching this conclusion because no one is talking to them about bringing science and faith into dialogue and integrating them into our worldview. It is our job as catechists to have this conversation and help them understand how to interpret Scripture in a way that recognizes the Bible's occasional inclusion of allegorical or nonliteral genres. At the same time, when we encounter the use of figurative language in Scripture, such as we see in the creation stories of Genesis, we must not dismiss them as mere fairy tales but rather as vehicles of divine truth.

Scripture

But you, remain faithful to what you have learned and believed, because you know from whom you learned it, and that from infancy you have known [the] sacred scriptures, which are capable of giving you wisdom for salvation through faith in Christ Jesus. All scripture is inspired by God and is useful for teaching, for refutation, for correction, and for training in righteousness. 2 TIMOTHY 3:14–16

Prayer

Help me, Lord, to better know you through the stories of Scripture so that I may be filled with your wisdom. Guide me in using the stories and illustrations of Scripture in my sessions so that those I teach will be trained in righteousness and will learn the way that leads to salvation. Amen.

Chapter Fifteen

Power Tools: Using Technology

If a construction crew arrived to remodel your home and you noticed that they didn't have any power tools at their disposal, you would question whether they could get the job done. Similarly, today's learners question the relevance and significance of educational or formational experiences that do not incorporate technology to some degree.

> **Failing adequately to consider [digital] phenomena leads to the risk of appearing insignificant to many people.**
>
> —*Directory for Catechesis*, 213

I'll never forget the day in 1973 when my eighth-grade teacher Sr. Laurenta wheeled into our classroom a cart holding a huge reel-to-reel videotape machine that she used to record us doing presentations. We were fascinated by this cutting-edge device that enabled us to immediately see ourselves in action. The immediate feedback it provided made us more interested in our learning.

In the twenty-first century, learners, especially young people, expect technology to be part of the learning experience.

In the twenty-first century, learners, especially young people, expect technology to be part of the learning experience. And that includes faith formation. While it is an exaggeration to say that the medium is the message, it is, in fact, true that the medium affects how the message is perceived and received.

What Did Aquinas and Augustine Do without Technology?

Back when I was teaching religion in a Catholic high school, I recall requesting a TV/VCR at the last moment for my class. The exasperated librarian sighed deeply and asked, "What did Aquinas and Augustine do without technology?"

It's true that for centuries the Church's greatest teachers accomplished wonderful things without the assistance of a kilowatt of electricity. By the same token, they used whatever was state of the art in their day. The invention of the printing press in the fifteenth century had profound implications on the spread of the gospel. As literacy became increasingly widespread, the written word came to be just as crucial as the spoken word, which once seemed sufficient. In today's digital world, images, which used to be thought of as simply enhancing the text on a page, are now considered more crucial than the written word!

In the twenty-first century, young people interact with a wide array of technologies before they even learn to walk. Our learners are digital natives who are fluent in technological language, while some of us catechists are still digital immigrants striving to grasp and understand technologies that our learners take for granted. In educational settings, young people are accustomed to being engaged throughout the day by various forms of technology. Catechists, likewise, must strive to utilize digital tools and various forms of technology that can assist in effectively proclaiming the Good News of Jesus Christ in the twenty-first century.

In the twenty-first century, young people interact with a wide array of technologies before they even learn to walk.

"My life was changed in Sunday school... and that was before we even had overhead projectors."

Be Not Afraid

Before we go any further, however, let me stress that you do not have to become a technological genius to excel as a twenty-first century catechist, nor do your lessons and faith formation experiences need to become fully digitized and technology-based. The truth is, most catechists do not even have access to the kinds of technology that are now standard in school settings. This does not excuse us, however, from incorporating some form(s) of technology into our faith formation setting, even if it is nothing more than the occasional use of your own cell phone or tablet, an LCD projector, and a portable Bluetooth speaker. Digital technology is an integral part of twenty-first century culture.

We live in a knowledge-based society that is rapidly becoming more complex, interconnected, and accelerated. The bottom line is that the more tools we use to proclaim the Good News of Jesus Christ, the more likely the message will be heard. We must constantly reimagine the methods by which we proclaim the gospel. With that in mind, let's look at some things to consider when it comes to using technology in faith formation.

> In essence, using technology in faith formation is a form of inculturation—of meeting people where they are.

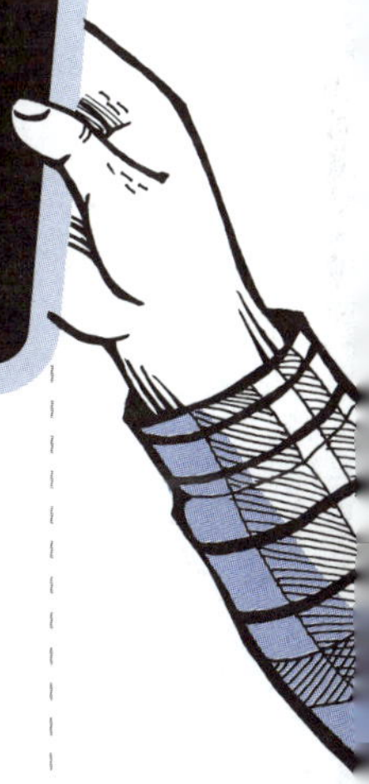

- **Decide on the Most Effective Medium for Your Lesson**—Don't let the tail wag the dog. The technology you use must fit in with your learning outcomes if it is to be effective. The goal is not simply to use technology but rather to make disciples of Christ while relying on some form of technology as a tool. One does not use a power hammer to sand a piece of wood. Be sure your selection of technology will help you achieve your lesson's learning outcomes.
- **Continually Familiarize Yourself with New Technologies**—One of the simplest ways to keep abreast of the kind of technologies being used in education is to ask your learners what their teachers are using in school. When our granddaughter was in kindergarten, she asked my wife, "Grandma, do you know what a SMART Board is?" She went on to describe what it is and how her teacher was using it to engage them. Kids are more than happy to

> **Do not be afraid of new technologies!**
> —St. Pope John Paul II

tell you about the latest "toys" they are using in education. You can also participate in catechetical workshops where presenters offer workshops on using digital technology in faith formation.

- **Build Your Digital Technological Vocabulary**—Sometimes, when you listen to a conversation about digital technology and hear words such as avatar, vodcast, bandwidth, synchronous versus asynchronous, and open-source software, it's hard not to feel as though folks are speaking a foreign language! Again, you don't need to learn every new word or phrase that comes from the digital continent; however, it is helpful to have some familiarity with the digital vocabulary that your learners are using on a regular basis.

- **Low-Tech Is Still Tech**—In my experience, the average catechist has access to very little in the way of digital technology in their learning space, and few catechetical programs are able to provide tablets for their learners (whereas many Catholic schools are able to provide them). For that reason, I am being careful in this chapter not to overwhelm you with a myriad of innovative digital technologies. In fact, I will do the opposite and identify what I consider to be the five most basic digital capabilities expected of a catechist.

  - **Play music using your smartphone and a portable Bluetooth speaker.** Throughout this book, I've emphasized the importance of implementing music in faith formation, and digital technology makes it easy for you to do just that. Simply identify songs you wish to use, download them to a playlist on your smartphone, and play them through a portable Bluetooth speaker, which can be amplified to fill a good-size space.
  - **Scan QR codes in your catechetical textbook or leader guide to show or view videos.** As I mentioned previously, faith formation programs such as *Finding God* and *Christ Our Life* (Loyola Press) include QR codes in the children's text and catechist guide. You can have learners use their own smartphones to scan QR codes and view brief videos that reinforce the lesson, or you can scan the code and show it on your tablet if you have a small enough group. For larger groups, you'll simply need to connect your tablet to an LCD projector.

- **Use an LCD projector for slide presentations and videos.** Speaking of LCD projectors, you may have access to a built-in projector in your learning space, or your catechetical leader may be able to provide you with one so that you can show videos and slide presentations to enhance your lesson. You may also consider acquiring your own Bluetooth LCD mini projector for an easy, wireless connection. Today's learners are very visual, so be sure to learn how to use this technology to keep them engaged.
- **Use smartphones to access specific information and to record videos.** Rather than banning smartphones in your learning space, turn them into learning tools that your learners can use to access specific information (articles, wikis, websites, videos, traditional prayers, Catholic practices, saints, Church history) that will enhance your lesson. With content being so readily accessible, you no longer need to be the font of all knowledge or the sole delivery system of content. Put your learners to work by sending them to reputable, approved sites where they will access information that they will then share with the group. If not every learner has a smartphone, have them work in pairs. Likewise, use smartphones to record videos of your learners giving presentations, performing role-plays, and sharing with the group so that you can share the videos with parents.

Rather than banning smartphones in your learning space, turn them into learning tools.

- **Use smartphones or your computer or tablet to tap into your publisher's digital resources.** Catechetical publishers (such as Loyola Press) provide numerous digital resources for catechists, learners, and parents. You can direct learners to use their smartphones, or you can use your computer or tablet to access review games that will reinforce learning in a fun way.

Bonus Idea: Use Smartphones and QR Codes for Scavenger Hunts

You can create scavenger hunts that rely on QR codes. For example, arrange a scavenger hunt tour of the church without even leaving your learning space! Take pictures of the areas, objects, vessels, and vestments you want learners to become familiar with. Caption each photo with a brief description. Upload the photos to a sharing platform. Then use a free online QR generator to create a QR code for each link. Post the QR codes in your learning space and direct the learners to use their smartphones to scan each one to compile a complete list that will help build their liturgical vocabulary.

You don't have to use every one of these digital technologies in every session. However, I encourage you to incorporate them whenever possible and when most useful in order to truly speak the language used by your learners.

Teaching in a Virtual Setting

Scan this QR code to view a brief video of Joe offering tips on doing faith formation in a virtual environment.

Something Good Came Out of the Pandemic?

While few of us have any good memories of the COVID-19 pandemic, one good thing that came out of that experience was that many previously reluctant Catholic catechetical ministers found it necessary to finally wade ashore onto the digital continent as they found themselves suddenly having to teach virtually. And, while virtual faith formation has its drawbacks and is not ideal for all circumstances, many catechists today continue to effectively facilitate faith formation gatherings in virtual settings for learners who are either unable to attend in person or who simply find it more convenient to participate virtually.

The Internet and Social Media—The Internet provides you and your learners with almost unlimited access to quality Catholic information and resources that can serve your lessons. Consider the following:

- Check with your catechetical leader to determine if Internet access is available in your learning space; be sure to acquire any needed usernames and passwords to gain access.
- Be extraordinarily careful about sending your learners to surf the Internet for information. Make sure you have researched any Web sites you want them to visit to ensure that all of the information on that site is acceptable.
- When working with children, make sure parents are aware of any Internet assignments you have given.
- You can use social media to send links and communications to your learners and their parents that will reinforce, enhance, and help them live out what you are teaching. By providing these materials online, you provide your learners with increased flexibility and opportunities for learning.
- Check your diocesan Web site for links to quality Catholic sites. Be aware that many Web sites using the name *Catholic* are not necessarily reliable or authentically Catholic.

A catechist was using a computer for the first time to do a presentation with her second graders when suddenly the computer stopped working. Unable to reboot the computer, the catechist asked rhetorically, "What on earth happened?" A second grader sitting right next to the computer replied, "It's obvious: the hard drive crashed." The catechist got on the intercom to the office and said, "Can you please send another computer to my room? The hard drive crashed on this one." The office helper was skeptical that the catechist would know how to accurately diagnose the problem correctly and said, "How can you be so sure that the problem is the hard drive?" The catechist replied, "One of the second graders told me." The office helper responded, "I'm so sorry I doubted you. I'll send another one down immediately."

Pope St. John Paul II referred to mass media, including the Internet, as the "first Areopagus of the modern age" (*Redemptoris missio*, 37c). The Areopagus was a public meeting place in ancient Athens where ideas could be freely expressed, exchanged, and debated. Be sure to guide your learners into "today's Areopagus" so that they learn how to engage with the world about their faith.

- Also, check with your parish catechetical leader and your diocese to make sure that you are aware of and compliant with any policies related to Internet and social media use in faith formation.

Technology will never replace great teachers, but technology in the hands of great teachers is transformational.

—George Couras

Scripture

The churches of Asia send you greetings. Aquila and Prisca together with the church at their house send you many greetings in the Lord. All the brothers greet you. Greet one another with a holy kiss. I, Paul, write you this greeting in my own hand. 1 Corinthians 16:19–21

Prayer

St. Paul was the first to use the medium of the letter to spread the gospel of Jesus. Today, there are so many tools available to use in preaching your word, Lord. Help me be as innovative as St. Paul. Help me best utilize technology in my lessons so that I may capture the imagination of my learners and bring the power of your word to life. Amen.

Chapter Sixteen

Tape Measures: Assessing Progress

When cutting any kind of materials, it's wise to follow the advice to measure twice, cut once. The precision of a digital caliper, for example, eliminates guesswork and provides error-free measurements. In faith formation, it is important for catechists to measure (assess) the progress of learners as they embrace a life of discipleship.

> **The pedagogical formation of the catechist should develop several attitudes in him, including . . . the capacity to . . . make an assessment.**
>
> —*Directory for Catechesis*, 149e

Do You Understand?

Jesus often assessed his disciples' understanding of what he had said or done. For example, after he washed the feet of the apostles, Jesus said, "Do you realize what I have done for you?" (John 13:12). After teaching many parables, Jesus asked his disciples, "Do you understand all these things?" (Matthew 13:51). When Jesus warned his disciples about the "yeast of the Pharisees" and the disciples argued about what that meant, Jesus asked, "Do you not yet understand?" (Matthew 16:9). Jesus did not hesitate to assess his disciples' understanding of his teaching.

> **Jesus often assessed his disciples' understanding of what he had said or done.**

For some reason, however, when it comes to our faith formation efforts, there is a tendency to shy away from measuring or assessing where disciples are on their journey. While it is improper to give a test to determine if someone can receive a sacrament, or for the purpose of deciding whether a learner has passed or failed a faith formation experience, the fact is, we *are* responsible for assessing the progress of learners on their faith formation journey. Such assessment, however, involves much more than simply giving an exam.

> **Good teachers know how to bring out the best in students.**
> —Charles Kuralt

"There Must Be Evidence"

The Order of Christian Initiation for Adults (OCIA), which serves as the model for all catechesis, states clearly that catechists and pastoral staff are responsible for discerning the readiness of catechumens and candidates. For example, in anticipation of the Rite of Acceptance and Welcoming, OCIA paragraph 42 explicitly states:

> "The prerequisite for making this step is that the beginnings of the spiritual life and the fundamentals of Christian teachings have taken root in the candidate. There must be evidence of the first faith . . . of an initial conversion and intention to change their lives and to enter into a relationship with God in Christ."

We Have the Responsibility to Assess

The OCIA says that pastoral teams "have the responsibility for judging the outward indications of such dispositions." Again, such assessment is not accomplished by simply giving a test. However, it does involve determining the extent to which a developing disciple has had a conversion of heart and mind, has embraced new practices or actions, and has acquired new knowledge and skills to serve the mission of Christ.

Paragraph 43 goes on to say: "Before the Rite is celebrated, therefore, sufficient and necessary time . . . should be set aside to evaluate and, if necessary, to purify the candidates' motives and dispositions."

You've Changed

Think about it. When someone makes a new commitment in their life (starting a new job, beginning life together in marriage, embracing sobriety), that commitment is evidenced by a change in their actions, their appearance, the way(s) they spend their time, and who they spend their time with. Similarly, in faith formation, assessment should be looking for not only knowledge but also evidence of new behaviors. In doing so, we can help individuals measure the extent to which they are embracing the lifestyle of discipleship, as well as the extent to which our teaching is helping them do this. In other words, assessment says as much about the teacher as it does about the learner.

Assessment says as much about the teacher as it does about the learner.

Assessment *Is* Accompaniment

Assessment (from the Latin *assidere,* meaning "to sit with") is something we do *with* and *for* a learner, not *to* a learner. We are not only assessing *their* comprehension of key concepts but also *our* effectiveness in transmitting those concepts. In essence, assessment is a form of accompaniment. We seek to assess the formation that is taking place in our learners and offer feedback leading to further growth. Since people learn in a variety of ways, a variety of forms of assessment are needed. Let's look at some examples.

If we are to teach as Jesus did, we must constantly be assessing, in a variety of forms, whether his present-day followers are grasping the knowledge and skills needed to be a disciple in today's world.

- **Informal or Formative Assessment**—Refers to the ongoing monitoring of learning to provide ongoing feedback that can help teachers adjust their teaching and learners improve their comprehension. This type of assessment mirrors what Jesus did after he sent seventy-two disciples out in pairs to proclaim the kingdom. Upon their return, Jesus gathered them to hear their reports and to assess their progress (Luke 10:1–24).
    - **Ongoing**—Include opportunities to assess your learners' grasp of concepts by observing their participation in discussions, group work, prayer and reflection, and service to others.
    - **Specific Tasks**—Include specific opportunities to evaluate verbal (oral and written) and nonverbal (drawn, crafted, presented) expressions and responses. In addition to occasional quizzes or tests, these may take the shape of activities that invite your learners to express in a variety of forms their understanding or application of various concepts.

The Bishop Would Like to Ask a Few Questions

In faith formation, interviews done as a form of assessment take inspiration from and should be modeled after the questions asked by the bishop at the Rite of Election to guide the discernment of the extent to which an individual is growing in "intimate knowledge of the Mystery of salvation" (OCIA, 131B).

- "Have they faithfully listened to God's word proclaimed by the Church?"
- "Have they begun to walk in God's presence, treasuring the word they have received?"
- "Have they persevered in the communion of the faithful and in the prayers?"

Formal or Summative Assessments—Refers to assessment done at the end of an instructional period (a chapter, unit, liturgical season) and in relation to a set of standards or benchmarks that gives learners the opportunity to demonstrate what they have learned as well as what they can do with what they've learned. In addition to some form of test, quiz, or exam, formal assessment can take the shape of the following:

- **Service Experiences**—Provide suggestions for specific ways that your learners can put their faith into practice by serving others, either individually or as a group, and then reflect on the impact of that experience on their faith journey.
- **Interviews**—A good way to conduct assessment is through an interview, not to be confused with an oral exam. In other words, the interview is not just asking questions to test a learner's recall. Rather, it is an authentic conversation. In recent decades, many faith formation programs have taken to doing interviews with their confirmandi before reception of the sacrament. This same approach can be used in any faith formation experience or setting.
- **Learner Portfolios**—A portfolio is a collection of a learner's work over a period of time. Portfolios are a means for allowing learners to see the arc of their growth and progress. Portfolios also give catechists the opportunity to gain insight into their learners' efforts, progress, achievements, and thought processes, as well as their strengths and needs. One of the advantages of using portfolios is that learners are actively engaged in their own ongoing assessment. However, catechists need to help learners identify portfolio-worthy assignments (see the QR code on the next page for suggestions). File folders or binders can be used as portfolios because it is easy for learners to add or take work out of them over time. Learners should have easy access to their portfolios and should be encouraged to interact with their portfolios often.

Sample Interview Questions

Here are some sample interview questions that can be adjusted for various age groups:

- What words would you use to describe your relationship with God?
- What made the most impact on you in this year's faith formation experience?
- What do you find most inspiring about the Catholic faith?
- How has your faith grown in the past year?
- What challenges your faith?
- How have you changed as a follower of Jesus?
- What helps to deepen your relationship with God?
- When and how do you experience prayer?
- What is your favorite Gospel story? Why?
- If you were asked to explain who Jesus is to a group of people who do not know him, how would you describe him?
- Who is a good Catholic role model for you? How does this person inspire you?
- Where and how do you find God in your life?
- What does receiving Jesus in the Eucharist mean to you?
- In what ways have you been of service to others?
- Who is a saint that inspires you? Why?
- In what area(s) of your life do you most need God's grace right now?
- What role does Scripture (God's word) play in your life? How can this grow?
- In what way(s) is God calling you to change and grow?

Scan this QR code to view a brief video of Joe sharing examples of portfolio-worthy assignments.

Breaking Out of the "Final Exam" Mentality

It is no secret that, for the last couple of centuries, the Church's approach to faith formation in the United States has been based on an academic model. One of the vestiges of this model is the notion of a final exam. When it comes to assessment, we immediately think of an exam. Let's remember, however, that we are not teaching a subject but are facilitating encounters with Christ. This calls for a different kind of assessment.

We are not teaching a subject but are facilitating encounters with Christ.

Any approach to assessment in faith formation must pay attention to the various ways that people learn and prefer to express themselves, which means that we must offer options for learners. Based on what we covered in chapter 6 about various learning styles, here are some options by which learners can demonstrate (not only to you, but also, if you choose, to the rest of the group, a group of younger learners, or even the parish-at-large) their comprehension, grasp, and significance of what they have learned while also giving them the opportunity to be true disciples and to spread the Good News:

- film a video of themselves
- compose and perform or record a song
- participate in an interview
- create and present a lesson
- write a summary, poem, essay, or story
- draw or paint a picture or series of pictures (e.g., a triptych)
- design a poster, pamphlet, or digital presentation
- design a Web site
- draw stained glass windows
- create a comic strip
- perform a dance
- create an exhibit
- perform a role play or dramatized story
- create a *visio divina* experience
- make a photo montage of their faith journey
- deliver a slide presentation to the group

- deliver a speech
- create, participate in, or facilitate a "game"
- create a scavenger hunt using QR codes
- build something
- create an ad or commercial
- work with a partner on any of the above

And Yes, There *Is* a Place for Testing in Faith Formation

Throughout this chapter, we have downplayed the use of quizzes, tests, and exams as a form of assessment in faith formation to reinforce the fact that we are not teaching a subject but are facilitating encounters with Christ. Having said that, the fact is, God's saving grace has been revealed to us throughout salvation history through specific words and actions. For this reason, it is imperative that disciples of Christ can draw on this specific content to better understand their faith and to talk about their faith with others.

> **Teaching is more than imparting knowledge; it is inspiring change.**
> —William Arthur Ward

In other words, we have every right to assess the extent to which learners are embracing and comprehending content in faith formation—with these important caveats:

- Assessments are not intended to determine a grade (or a determination of pass/fail) but rather to indicate which concepts need further attention or which learners need further instruction.
- We must never rely on quizzes or tests either to determine eligibility for a sacrament or to pass/fail learners; rather, assessments are given to indicate how to better accompany the learner on their journey.

If I have to face a test of faith, I'd prefer a written exam.

Keep the Following in Mind

When using quizzes or tests in faith formation, keep the following in mind:

- Make sure that the items included on your quizzes or tests are consistent with the learning outcomes for your lesson.
- Provide your learners with opportunities for self-assessment. In other words, ask them to identify specific concepts they understand as well as specific concepts they have questions about and need more help to understand.
- Make sure that learners are given the opportunity and direction to find correct answers for items they responded to incorrectly.
- Invite learners to identify concepts that they are having difficulty with.
- Provide prompt feedback on quizzes and tests and offer suggestions for how to improve.

Assessment: You Will Know Them by Their Fruits

After his conversion on the road to Damascus, Saul faced the challenge of convincing the Christian community that he was now Paul, a follower of the risen Christ. At the same time, the Christian community faced the challenge of assessing the validity of this man's conversion, given the fact that he once sought to have them exterminated. We are told that Paul spent time with the other apostles, learning from them and, no doubt, being assessed by them. It wasn't an exam that Paul aced that convinced the Christian community to accept him. It was his words and actions that provided the evidence of his authenticity. As you consider your approach to assessment in faith formation, keep this question in mind: What words and actions indicate that this learner is growing in a life of discipleship?

A confirmation candidate received several critical remarks on an assessment his catechist had given. He went to speak to the catechist and said, "I think I deserve more credit, even if my answers weren't entirely correct." The catechist sighed and said, "Okay, I'll take another look at it and offer some remarks." When the learner went home, his mother asked, "So how did the assessment go?" He replied, "Awesome! My catechist thought it was remarkable."

Assessing Your Program's Effectiveness—The Assessment of Catechesis/Religious Education (ACRE), provided by the National Catholic Education Association (NCEA), is a formal assessment tool used to assess the extent to which learners are grasping concepts of our faith tradition, and make changes in their curriculum accordingly. ACRE is designed to be used with young people on three levels: fifth grade, eighth or ninth grade, and eleventh or twelfth grade. ACRE is not used to assess individuals but rather to evaluate the effectiveness of a catechetical program as a whole. Each site that uses ACRE receives a composite report that includes an analysis of participants' responses.

Scripture

So when he had washed their feet [and] put his garments back on and reclined at table again, he said to them, "Do you realize what I have done for you?" JOHN 13:12

Prayer

Lord Jesus, when you washed the feet of your disciples, you asked them if they understood what you had just done for them. You taught and then you assessed the extent to which your message had penetrated. Help me teach your word and also assess the effectiveness of my efforts so that I might know how to better invite my learners to learn the way of salvation. Amen.

Chapter Seventeen

Stud Finder: Connecting with Parents

A stud finder is used to locate framing studs found behind the surface of a wall so you can be certain you're hammering a nail or inserting a screw into something that will hold whatever you're attaching to the wall. In faith formation, unless we make a solid connection with parents, our efforts with children may not take hold.

> **Believing parents, with their daily example of life, have the most effective capacity to transmit the beauty of the Christian faith to their children. The greatest challenge [for parents] is to overcome the mentality of delegation that is so common, according to which the faith is set aside for specialists in religious education.**
>
> —*Directory for Catechesis*, 124

Will It Hold?

If you hammer a nail into drywall or paneling, but don't sink that nail into a wall stud, the nail may not be able to hold the weight of the frame or shelf you hope to place there. It is important to fasten that nail through the wall and into the wall stud, which serves as a solid foundation. When it comes to forming children in faith, we know all too well that what we teach them will not hold without the solid support of their parents. One of the biggest frustrations that catechists face is the lack of parental support in children's faith formation.

"This is our son, Shawn. We'll be back to pick him up when he turns eighteen."

Now, before we go all nuclear on today's parents, let's recognize that the system we are operating in—Catholic children's faith formation—has for decades asked parents to be little more than chauffeurs. For too long, we have given the message that all they need to do is drop off the kids and we (the parish) will form them in faith. While this may have worked in bygone eras when Catholic families lived in insular communities where Catholicism was lived and breathed by seemingly everyone, that world is gone.

Catholic children's faith formation has for decades asked parents to be little more than chauffeurs.

The End of the Catholic Bubble

Like many Catholics of my generation (I was born in 1959), I grew up in a Catholic bubble—a close-knit community where Catholics, usually of the same ethnic background, clustered together and practiced their faith tradition. I grew up thinking the whole world was Catholic. With such a supportive infrastructure, faith formation could be completed with the old reliable *Baltimore Catechism*, a set of questions and answers to provide children with the words they needed to articulate Catholic doctrine. In other words, since the family and community formed children in the faith tradition, we could rely on a system in which parents could drop off their kids to get their catechism in a one-size-fits-all approach.

That world no longer exists. An "ecology of institutions" (John H. Westerhoff III, *Will Our Children Have Faith?*) that once supported a life of faith has evaporated. In the early-to-middle twentieth century . . .

- **. . . Catholics lived in primarily homogenous, insular, stable communities** in which people held shared traditions and values, and everyone was committed (and equipped) to forming their children in faith. Today's world and the communities that many people live in are much more diverse, pluralistic, and fragmented, and families, themselves often fragmented, are more mobile than ever before.
- **. . . most children came home to at least one parent** (usually the mom), and oftentimes also grandparents, who made it their responsibility to teach faith traditions and practices, including family devotions and piety. Today, with most parents working full-time and with young people involved in after-school activities, parents and children have less time together.

- **. . . public schools supported and mirrored Christian values,** including Christian prayer, Bible reading, and moral and religious lessons in the classroom. In fact, Catholic schools were developed in response to public schools that Catholic leaders viewed as publicly funded Protestant schools. As a result of landmark Supreme Court decisions in the early 1960s that struck down school-sponsored prayer, public schools became less and less overtly Christian.
- **. . . the authority of the Church was unquestioned by Catholics,** and the parish was the hub of social life. This, of course, was before widespread knowledge of the clergy sex abuse scandal. Today, people in general have much less trust in the authority of institutions, and this applies to how many Catholics view Church authority. The days of "pay, pray, and obey" are gone, which means that Church teachings no longer go unquestioned in Catholic households.

In addition to the erosion of respect for Church authority, people no longer look to parishes to provide social engagement and entertainment when those realities can be found elsewhere in more robust forms.

- **. . . families were able to control the flow of information into their homes.** With one phone, a radio, a TV, a newspaper, and a few magazines, parents were able to control what their children were exposed to. Today, with children carrying their own cell phones, parents have little control over the information that their children can encounter at the touch of a finger.

Today, with children carrying their own cell phones, parents have little control over the information that their children can encounter at the touch of a button.

- **. . . Sundays were sacred** with few or no conflicts from sports or other activities. In other words, churchgoing had little to no competition, and with people living in Catholic bubbles, one's absence at church on Sunday was easily noticed. Today, the sanctity of Sunday has all but disappeared, with children involved in sports and other activities, stores and entertainment being open and available, and parents themselves often working. Churchgoing, especially in the post-pandemic era, has become just one more activity.

You and I know that today, this "ecology of institutions" that once served as an infrastructure for faith formation is gone. As a result, too many of our faith formation efforts are like trying to hang a heavy frame on a nail that is not secured into the wall stud, and it all comes crashing down. The answer lies ahead. In the words of Donna Toliver Grimes, "The time has come to release the notion of a 'Catholic bubble' which, in reality, no longer exists. Like Tom Hanks' character in the film, *Cast Away*, now is the right time to say, 'Goodbye, Wilson!'" (*All God's People*).

I am convinced that the very foundations upon which we engage in Christian education are shaking.
—John H. Westerhoff III

Is God's Language Spoken at Home?

Linguistics experts tell us that the primary factor in a child learning a new language is exposure to that new language, and that the greatest exposure possible is when that language is spoken at home. This explains why my efforts at learning Spanish have not been as successful as I hoped; I have very little exposure to Spanish since it is not spoken in my home or at work. Much of what I learn simply gets lost because it is not being reinforced.

A mother was enjoying the newsletters she'd been receiving from the parish catechetical leader, offering tips on how to speak to their children about faith. One morning, as she was making pancakes for her sons, the boys began to argue over who would get the first pancake. The mom saw the opportunity for a moral lesson. "If Jesus were sitting here, he would say, 'Let my brother have the first pancake; I can wait.' The older brother turned to his younger brother and said, "Let's role play. You be Jesus."

The same holds true of our faith formation efforts. It is as if we are trying to teach children a new language—God's language, a language of faith—when that language is rarely spoken at home. It is critical that we help parents speak God's language at home so that their children's faith formation will be reinforced by the most important people in their lives. Let's look at some suggestions:

It is critical that we help parents speak God's language at home.

- Encourage parents to speak God's language at home and offer tips and opportunities for how to create a climate or culture of faith at home:
  - Pray regularly as a family, especially at mealtime.
  - Allow your children to catch you doing something related to your faith (praying the rosary, reading the Bible or other Catholic literature, participating in a service experience or ministry at the parish).
  - Place a Bible and other sacred objects such as a crucifix or an icon of Mary in the home.
  - Observe the Church's liturgical calendar (seasons and feasts) at home.
  - Learn about and engage in Catholic practices (blessing their children, fasting, wearing a scapular or cross around their neck, praying a novena).
  - Practice virtues and talk openly about the struggle to be a virtuous person in today's world.
  - Attend Mass regularly and sit right up in front so that children can be more engaged in the Mass.
  - Read Bible stories and stories of the lives of the saints to children.
  - Do service together as a family and talk about the experience.
- In cooperation with your catechetical leader, call or send a text or e-mail to the parents of each child in your group, introducing yourself and inviting parents to reach out to you if they have any questions. As an option, consider hosting a ten-minute virtual meeting to introduce yourself to parents.

A Weekly Take-Home Page or Packet

When I served as a catechist of sixth graders and then fourth graders, I arranged for a folder to go home weekly, with a page attached to the children's work that parents were asked to sign and have the children return the following week. Each week, the first thing we did was to check on those returns. By doing so, we eventually had about 80 percent cooperation from parents. Instead of sending textbooks home, tear out specific pages to send home in a folder with the above-mentioned cover page for parents to sign and return.

- Emphasize and send home any "family pages" in your catechetical textbook or resources, and encourage learners to engage with their parents in any activities suggested on those resources.
- Consider creating a cover page that gets stapled to anything that goes home to the parents and requires them to sign and return to verify that they have indeed received and reviewed the communication.

> **Children have never been very good at listening to their elders, but they have never failed to imitate them.**
>
> —James Baldwin

- Arrange an e-mail or text messaging system through your catechetical leader that permits you to send occasional messages to parents summarizing what their children have learned and including important communications for the parents. Ask for replies and for them to confirm receipt of your e-mails and texts.

Come On In

Many parish catechetical leaders have established a policy requiring parents to enter the building and go to their child's classroom at dismissal time from religious education. This gives catechists some time to connect personally with parents while, at the same time, providing for greater safety of children at dismissal time.

Parents Are Key

Research consistently shows that learning is enhanced when children have parents who support and are involved in their learning. Likewise, research shows that teachers who work at building positive and strong home-school relationships are more effective. As catechists, we can never underestimate the influence that parents can and do have on their children's faith formation.

- Greet parents warmly every time you see them and engage them in conversation about their child. Ask parents for their help and advice as often as possible and as needed to better serve their children.

As catechists, we can never underestimate the influence that parents can and do have on their children's faith formation.

- Send home weekly notes that keep them informed of what their children are learning and doing. Offer suggestions for fostering faith discussions at home. Send home the texts of any prayers the children are learning and ask the parents to help their children take the words to heart and to do so themselves.
- Share links to quality Catholic Web sites and good Catholic content, including your publisher's Web site, where they can engage in review games and other interactive activities with their child.
- Arrange for a family service experience that invites parents and children to work together in the service of others.
- Invite parents to a recital of sorts at the end of the catechetical year—a show-what-you-know event that provides parents with the opportunity to see their children express or demonstrate what they have learned and how they have grown in the past year, using one of the many suggestions for formal or summative assessment listed in the previous chapter.

- Create a schedule for parents to serve as catechist helpers for sessions throughout the year, much as parents volunteer (or are often assigned or required) to work at the refreshment stand at their child's sporting events.
- If a child misses a session because of illness, contact the parents to ask how the child is doing and assure them that you and the children prayed for their child at the last session.
- Be a presence at activities that the children participate in such as sports, dance, recitals, etc., and use the opportunities to talk to parents. Do likewise for wakes and funerals, if possible, to show your care and concern to the family.
- Send thank you notes for any gifts you receive as well as for any other acts of kindness the parents have shown, such as volunteering to assist with a faith formation activity.
- Offer tips and support to parents on issues beyond faith themes to show the connection between life and faith.
- Create tote bags or take-home kits for families with resources to assist them in praying as a family, engaging in faith discussions, and even playing games associated with learning about their Catholic faith.
- Recommend faith-themed videos that the family can watch together.
- Constantly invite parents and families to participate in various parish activities and happenings and provide them with incentives for attending.

Don't worry that children never listen to you; worry that they are always watching you.
—Robert Fulghum

Don't Overlook Grandparents

For many families, it is the grandparents who carry out a special role in transmitting the Catholic faith to their grandchildren. When families are facing various crises or challenges, it is often the grandparents who step in and step up to be a source of strength, support, and wisdom. In many families, it is the grandparents who are more deeply rooted in the Catholic faith, and who assume the responsibility of raising the children in faith. Many people can point to their grandparents as being the primary influence in their faith development. Even Scripture points to the importance of the role of grandparents in faith formation: "As I recall your sincere faith that first lived in your grandmother Lois and in your mother Eunice and that I am confident lives also in you" (2 Timothy 1:5). As a catechist, don't overlook grandparents, who can serve a pivotal role in apprenticing young people into the faith.

Family Catechesis

Scan this QR code to access information about a family catechesis approach using faith formation programs such as *Finding God* and *Christ Our Life* (by Loyola Press).

Invite and Communicate

When it comes to connecting with parents, the most crucial words to remember are *invite* and *communicate*. Be sure that all the ways you reach out to parents have a sincerely hospitable (rather than a "bossy") tone. Always position yourself as a supportive partner. When it comes to communicating with parents, never underestimate the power of making connections. While you are most interested in teaching their children, please know that ultimately it is their parents who will have the most impact on them. The teachings that you are attempting to impress upon children will have a better chance of taking hold if parents are positioned to firmly anchor them.

Scripture

Take to heart these words which I command you today. Keep repeating them to your children. Recite them when you are at home and when you are away, when you lie down and when you get up. Deuteronomy 6:6–7

Prayer

Good and gracious God, your servant Moses taught parents to impress your word on their children. Grant that, as a catechist, I may partner with parents to impress upon their children the Good News of your Son, Jesus Christ. Help me support and work with parents to ensure that they and their children allow your word to be inscribed upon their hearts. Amen.

Chapter Eighteen

Sharpeners: Keeping Your Edge

A few tools in your toolbox (for example, scissors, knives, saws, pruners, shears, hatchet, an axe, and drill bits) have blades or edges that need sharpening from time to time. Sharp tools are, quite simply, more efficient. As a catechist, it is important to stay sharp through ongoing formation.

> **The formation of catechists requires particular attention because the quality of pastoral initiatives is necessarily connected to the persons who bring them into being. Formation is an ongoing process that . . . helps the baptized person to take shape.**
>
> —*Directory for Catechesis*, 130, 131

Staying Sharp

For me, learning has become a lifelong endeavor. It is one of the things that keeps my mind sharp—and staying mentally sharp is critical for anyone, but especially so for those who teach. In his book *The 7 Habits of Highly Effective People*, Stephen R. Covey identifies the seventh habit as "Sharpen the Saw," and talks about the "principles of balanced self-renewal." Covey considered this habit to be the one that makes all the other habits possible because it takes care of the greatest tool you have: yourself! To "sharpen the saw" is to "invest" in oneself, thus enabling one to "move on an upward spiral of growth and change, of continuous improvement."

This habit of keeping sharp and continuously improving, so essential for catechists, is accomplished by participation in ongoing formation. A catechist should never stop growing. The truth is, most catechists have no formal training as teachers. Most catechists are not professional schoolteachers with training in methodology and pedagogical skills. Because of that, it is imperative that catechists engage in introductory formation, followed by ongoing formation.

A catechist should never stop growing.

Being Well-Rounded

If we are to successfully take on the challenges of catechizing in the twenty-first century, it is important that we catechists are well-formed and well-rounded. When we speak of someone being a well-rounded person, we are referring to the fact that this person is fully developed and possesses knowledge, capabilities, and skills in a wide range of areas. Catechists are most definitely called to be well-rounded! To that end, the *Directory for Catechesis* insists that catechist formation be "three dimensional," focusing on the following three areas:

Intellectual growth should commence at birth and cease only at death.
—Albert Einstein

This Can't Be the End!

I remember standing last in line for graduation at the University of St. Mary of the Lake/Mundelein Seminary, waiting for diplomas to be awarded in hierarchical order for the many various degree programs the school offers, with Doctor of Ministry being last. As I stood there waiting to hear my name called, I heard the announcement, "And finally, the candidates for the Doctor of Ministry degree—the *terminal degree* of the University." I laughed to myself because that phrase—*terminal degree*—seemed to imply that there was no more learning to be done. I found this particularly ironic since the biggest lesson I learned from completing my doctorate was the realization that there was still so much to be learned!

- **Being**—Formation in the area of *being* is designed to ensure that the catechist is growing and maturing as a human being who can truly act as a witness of faith—a person possessing healthy emotional balance, the ability to relate well to others, a deepening spirituality, and the ability to think soundly and critically.
- **Knowing**—Formation in the area of *knowing* is designed to ensure that the catechist is capable of faithfully transmitting the Christian Tradition, which comes from familiarity with Scripture, the four pillars of the *Catechism of the Catholic Church*, the teachings of the Magisterium of the Church, and the faith development of those they are teaching.
- **Doing**—Formation in the area of *doing* (referred to in the *Directory for Catechesis* as "savoir-faire") is designed to ensure that the catechist is skilled in various methodologies and capable of effectively engaging those they teach in order to build relationships, effectively transmit the content of our faith, and facilitate the transformation of hearts and minds through prayerful encounters with Jesus Christ.

Let's take a closer look at all three dimensions of catechist formation to which you are called.

Being: The Right Stuff

Years ago, there was a movie called *The Right Stuff*, which told the story of the first American astronauts who piloted the Mercury 7 and the personal attributes and character traits they possessed that made them suitable for the pioneering task at hand. We refer to people having

Catechists are most definitely called to be well-rounded!

What If Salt Loses Its Flavor?

Jesus told his disciples that they were the "salt of the earth" but then reminded them that salt can go flat (Matthew 5:13). The word *flat* is rarely complimentary or positive. Food, singing, tires, feet, and sales that are *flat* are nothing to be excited about. As catechists, we are called to be well-rounded, not flat.

the right stuff as meaning that they have the necessary or ideal qualities or capabilities needed for a specific situation or task.

Catechists need to have the right stuff too if they are to be effective, and this means more than simply possessing encyclopedic knowledge of the faith or flashy teaching skills. It means being people who possess virtues and qualities that enable them to flourish as healthy human beings and authentic disciples of Christ. Even before we determine whether a potential catechist possesses sufficient knowledge and skills, we want to be sure that they are "put together" well.

Anyone who stops learning is old, whether at twenty or eighty. Anyone who keeps learning stays young.
—Henry Ford

Likewise, while a textbook or video can show how to pray the sign of the cross or recite traditional prayers, it cannot teach about developing an affective relationship with God. This can only be accomplished by a human being, namely the catechist. Only a human being can answer questions about life experience, guide conversation, tell personal stories, share feelings, empathize, or articulate the experience of mystery. Only a human being can lift up his or her heart to God and invite others to do the same. Only a human being can truly accompany another human being.

Therefore, the person of the catechist is crucial to the process of evangelization and catechesis. Serving as a catechist is a vocation—a calling from God. A vocation, like a plant, needs to be nurtured. Just as we make sure that a plant receives water, sunlight, and the nutrients it needs to grow and thrive, we also need to make sure that the vocation of each catechist is being nurtured.

A vocation, like a plant, needs to be nurtured.

Catechist formation, then, should help people to mature as human beings by strengthening positive traits and minimizing negative traits. It should help you as a catechist grow in the following areas:

- **Emotional health**—your ability to articulate feelings, attitudes, and values; awareness of personal gifts and limitations; self-care; ability to cope with stress; emotional balance; positivity; support systems; and sense of purpose

- **Critical thinking**—your open-mindedness, flexibility, clarity, articulation, reasoning, discernment of truth, awareness of biases, and ability to conceptualize, analyze, synthesize, and evaluate
- **Ability to relate to others in a healthy manner**—your healthy relationships, people skills, respect for boundaries, confidentiality, respect for all human beings, openness to diversity, and conflict management skills
- **Holiness**—your spiritual health, charity and compassion, capacity for self-reflection, personal and communal prayer, centrality of the Eucharist, imitation of Christ, and selflessness

Knowing: The Ability to Articulate

Too often, Catholics find themselves at a loss for words to describe specifically what God has revealed through his words and actions or to summarize, even in general terms, the narrative of salvation history. This is unfortunate, because the truth is our God has revealed himself and his plan for us through specific words and actions over the course of salvation history. A well-formed Christian should be able to articulate an understanding of that revelation.

For catechists, this is a crucial dimension of our formation: knowing. A catechist does not need to have an advanced degree in theology, but rather the ability to articulate a basic understanding of the Catholic faith (namely, the four pillars of our faith: creed, sacraments, morality, and prayer) and a basic understanding of the narrative of salvation history (and its central themes of, as I name them: rescue, restoration, and reassurance), which is climaxed in the Person of Jesus Christ.

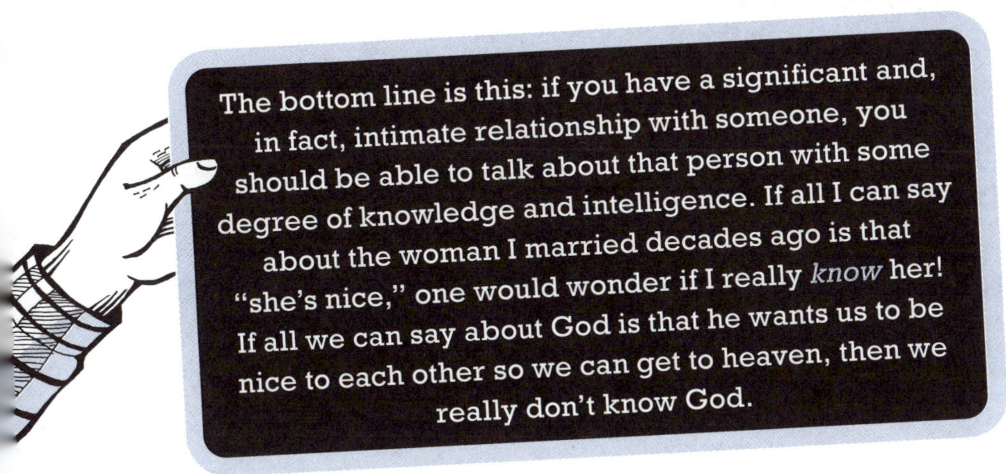

Faith Is More Than Being Nice

In their book *Soul Searching: The Religious and Spiritual Lives of American Teenagers*, Christian Smith and Melinda Lundquist Denton suggest that the "de facto dominant religion" among today's young people in the United States can be thought of as "Moralistic Therapeutic Deism." They surmise that this "religion" is characterized by the following beliefs:

- God exists.
- God wants people to be nice to each other.
- The goal of life is to be happy and to feel good about oneself.
- God is not too involved in our daily lives.
- Good people go to heaven when they die.

I think we would agree that our Catholic faith is a bit more substantive than this!

Catechist formation in the area of knowing should include the following:

- **Catholic doctrine**—Creed, Jesus, Church, Mary and the saints, the sacraments, liturgy, morality, social justice, Catholic social teaching, prayer, Scripture
- **Catechetical documents**—*Catechism of the Catholic Church, Directory for Catechesis, National Directory for Catechesis, Our Hearts Were Burning Within Us, Catechesi Tradendae, Renewing the Vision, Go and Make Disciples*
- **Papal encyclicals and apostolic letters**—*Redemptoris Missio, Deus Caritas Est, Evangelii Gaudium*
- **Catechetical models and resources**
- **Diocesan structures and local/national/international catechetical organizations**

"By the time he realized the danger, Carl had developed a compulsive chain-reference habit."

Doing: Savoir-Faire

One of my all-time favorite hockey players for the Chicago Blackhawks was Hall-of-Famer Denis Savard, known for his speed and finesse, which earned him the nickname of Savoir-Faire. We use this phrase to compliment people who can do what needs to be done and do it with confidence, poise, and flair. The *Directory for Catechesis* uses this term to refer to the third dimension of catechist formation, referring to the skills and techniques involved in getting the job done.

When I was in college, I decided I wanted to become a teacher, and I wanted to teach religion at a Catholic high school. To achieve this, I double-majored in theology and history, and I also minored in education for the purpose of achieving a teaching certificate for the state of Illinois. I did that because I wanted to excel not only in the *knowing* aspect of teaching but also in the *doing* aspect. Upon graduating, I was one of two people hired at a Catholic high school to teach religion, both of us with degrees in theology. However, as the year progressed, it was clear that the other new hire was struggling mightily in the classroom, namely because, while he was prepared in the *knowing* aspect of teaching, he had no training or preparation in the *doing* aspect.

When it comes to proclaiming the Good News of Jesus Christ, there are skills we as catechists can and must learn that will help us be more effective and engaging. However, most catechists are not professional teachers. It is for that reason that I have dedicated my life to helping catechists learn and master the skills needed to proclaim the gospel more effectively. This book, *The Catechist's Toolbox 2.0*, is your guide for doing—for becoming a catechist with savoir-faire! For a list of what skills and techniques should be included in catechist formation in the area of *doing*, just check out the Contents page of this book.

A catechist attended a workshop about effective storytelling. At his next session, he told the story of the Good Samaritan, in which a man was robbed, beaten, and left for dead. He described the situation in extremely vivid detail so his learners would be captured by the drama. Then he asked the group, "If you saw a person lying on the roadside all wounded and bleeding, what would you do?" After a few moments of silence, a little girl sheepishly said, "I think I'd throw up!"

License to Teach

In many states, to become a certified or licensed electrician, you are required to complete around eight thousand hours of work experience and around one hundred hours of classroom training. It makes sense, then, that dioceses require catechists to work toward certification by completing ongoing training and formation. After all, working with people's souls and the power of the Holy Spirit is simply working with another form of power and energy!

Doing Our Due Diligence

As noted above, it makes sense that, like electricians (and plumbers, and auto mechanics), catechists are required to work toward certification by completing ongoing training and formation. *The Catechist's Toolbox 2.0* by itself is not meant to be a substitute for formal catechetical formation and training. Rather, it serves as a complement to such preparation so that you can become the effective catechist that God is calling you to be. It is to this vocation that you have been called.

The Catechetical Formation Series

Scan this QR code to view a brief video of Joe offering information about *The Catechetical Formation Series*, an online catechist formation resource that he developed for Loyola Press.

Scripture

So, as you received Christ Jesus the Lord, walk in him, rooted in him and built upon him and established in the faith as you were taught, abounding in thanksgiving. COLOSSIANS 2:6–7

Prayer

Come, Holy Spirit, and fill my mind and heart with knowledge and wisdom that I may continue to grow as a catechist. Help me to *be* a healthy and holy disciple of Jesus, to *know* my faith, and to have the skills to *do* what is needed to effectively proclaim the kingdom of God to those I teach. Amen.

Conclusion: Am I Making a Difference?

Throughout this book, I have been making comparisons between tools used in home repair and the tools needed for effective catechesis. Many similarities exist. However, there is one major difference. Typically, when we complete some home repair, we can stand back and look at the final outcome and take satisfaction in the tangible results. As a catechist, your results will be much less tangible. How does one know when a life has been touched, a soul has been stirred, or a spirit has been ignited?

Most often you will not know the extent to which your efforts have been effective in transforming lives. In my own experience as a high school teacher, I recall a former student coming back to see me a few years after his graduation. He thanked me for a particular class session that I taught when he was a student. He said that it really came in handy now that he was in the workplace. I went home knowing that I had a good day some five or six years previous!

"Jeremy calls the class 'a smash hit!' Susan names it 'one of this year's best,' and I think it's destined to become a classic."

Many of us will never know what effect we have had on our learners. For this reason, it is all the more crucial to focus on acquiring the tools needed to be an effective catechist. The more refined our skills are, the more keenly aware we will be about the effectiveness of our efforts. The more specific we are about our own expectations of our learners, the more unambiguous and observable the results will be.

We may never know just how much we have touched the lives of our learners. But with the proper tools in our catechist's toolbox, we will leave our lessons knowing that, in some way, the word of God *has* touched their lives. In the end, we must realize that we are simply a tool in the hands of the Carpenter from Nazareth.

If God can work through me, he can work through anyone.
—St. Francis of Assisi

Bibliography

Barbour, Ian. *Religion and Science: Historical and Contemporary Issues.* San Francisco: HarperCollins, 1997.

Barone, John, and Charleen Katra. *The Adaptive Teacher: Faith-Based Strategies to Reach and Teach Learners with Disabilities.* Chicago: Loyola Press, 2019.

Benedict, Saint. *The Rule of St. Benedict.* Translated into English. A Pax Book, preface by W. K. Lowther Clarke. London: S.P.C.K., 1931.

Bloom, Benjamin. *Taxonomy of Educational Objectives, Handbook I: The Cognitive Domain.* New York: David McKay Co. Inc., 1956.

Catechism of the Catholic Church. 2nd ed. Vatican: Libreria Editrice, Vaticana, 2000.

Covey, Stephen. *The 7 Habits of Highly Effective People.* New York: Simon and Schuster, 1989.

Directory for Catechesis. Pontifical Council for the Promotion of the New Evangelization. Washington, D.C.: United States Conference of Catholic Bishops, 2020.

Gardner, Howard. *Multiple Intelligences SmartCard.* San Clemente, California: Kagan Publishing and Professional Development, 2002.

Grimes, Donna Toliver. *All God's People: Effective Catechesis in a Diverse Church.* The Catechetical Leader Series. Chicago: Loyola Press, 2017.

Groome, Thomas. *Christian Religious Education: Sharing Our Story and Vision.* San Francisco: Harper & Row, 1980.

Haidt, Jonathan, and Twenge, Jean M. "This Is Our Chance to Pull Teenagers Out of the Smartphone Trap," *The New York Times,* July 31, 2021.

Ignatius of Loyola, Saint. *The Spiritual Exercises of St. Ignatius*. 2nd ed. Translated by Louis J. Puhl, SJ. Chicago: Loyola Press, 2021.

National Directory for Catechesis. Pontifical Council for the Promotion of the New Evangelization. Washington, D.C.: United States Conference of Catholic Bishops, 2005.

Nelsen, Jane. *Positive Discipline: The Classic Guide to Helping Children Develop Self-Discipline, Responsibility, Cooperation, and Problem-Solving Skills*. New York: Ballantine Books, 2006.

Order of Christian Initiation of Adults: Ritual Edition. International Commission on English in the Liturgy, National Conference of Catholic Bishops. Collegeville, MN: Liturgical Press, 2024.

Our Hearts Were Burning Within Us: A Pastoral Plan for Adult Faith Formation in the United States. National Conference of Catholic Bishops. Washington, D.C.: USCCB Publishing, 1999.

Pope John Paul II. *Redemptoris Missio*. Washington, D.C.: United States Catholic Conference, 1990.

Sinek, Simon. "Why Good Leaders Make You Feel Safe." Filmed March 2014 at TED2014. TED video, 11:45. https://www.ted.com/talks/simon_sinek_why_good_leaders_make_you_feel_safe.

Smith, Christian, with Melinda Lundquist Denton. *Soul Searching: The Religious and Spiritual Lives of American Teenagers*. New York: Oxford University Press, 2005.

Twenge, Jean. *Generations: The Real Differences Between Gen Z, Millennials, Gen X, Boomers, and Silents—and What They Mean for America's Future*. New York: Atria Books, 2023.

Westerhoff III, John H. *Will Our Children Have Faith?* New York: Seabury Press, 1976.